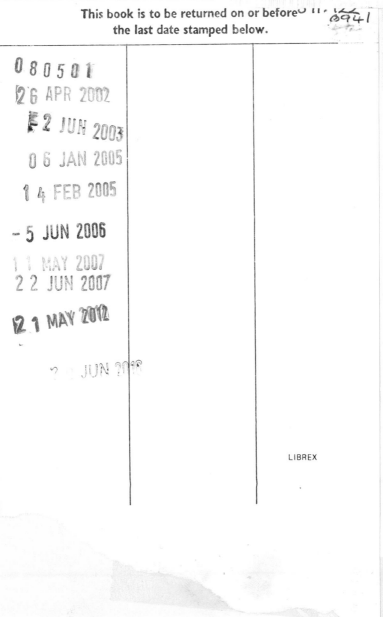

Issues in Education

Eric Hoyle and Peter John

Professional Knowledge and Professional Practice

CASSELL

Cassell
Villiers House
41/47 Strand
London WC2N 5JE

387 Park Avenue South
New York
NY 10016–8810

British Library Cataloguing-in-Publication Data
A catalogue record for this book is available from the
British Library.

ISBN: 0–304–32917–7 (hardback)
      0–304–32919–3 (paperback)

Typeset by Colset Private Limited, Singapore
Printed and bound in Great Britain by Biddles Ltd,
Guildford and King's Lynn

Contents

Foreword: the purpose of this series

The educational scene is changing rapidly. This change is being caused by a complexity of factors which includes a re-examination of present educational provision against a background of changing social and economic policies, new forms of testing and assessment, a National Curriculum, and local management of schools with more participation by parents.

As the educational process is concerned with every aspect of our lives and our society both now and for the future, it is of vital importance that all teachers, teachers in training, administrators and educational policy-makers should be aware and informed on current issues in education.

This series of books is thus designed to inform on current issues, to look at emerging ones, and to give an authoritative overview which will be of immense help to all those involved in the education process.

Philip Hills
Cambridge

1 The idea of a profession

Introduction

Profession is an essentially contested concept. Despite its
widespread use in the media and in the everyday discourse of
those who would be readily regarded as professional people,
and despite the best efforts of sociologists, philosophers and
historians, it defies common agreement as to its meaning. Professions are more easily instanced than defined, and dictionaries
tend to convey the meaning of the term more through example
than by identifying distinctive qualities. Where qualities are
cited these usually relate to *knowledge* and *responsibility*. The
professions are so consistently defined in terms of the possession
of knowledge that the term 'the learned professions' is a
pleonasm. The professions are perhaps less often defined in
terms of having a special responsibility to their clients, but this
is nevertheless the second most frequently cited defining feature.

It might be argued that if knowledge and responsibility are
generally accepted criteria, this would at least limit the contestability of the idea of a profession. This is to some extent
true, but there are those social theorists who doubt the distinc-
tiveness of the professions from other occupations precisely on
the grounds of just these two qualities. Doubts are frequently
expressed by politicians, pressure groups, and the clients of the
occupations so labelled. Even a number of those sociologists
who have spent their careers studying 'the professions' have
expressed their frustration at the intractability of the concept
and, if not actually advocating that its usage as a social science
concept should be abandoned, hold that it should at least be

hedged around with qualifying phrases and disclaimers. However, the term cannot be legislated out of existence by sociologists, since as a concept-in-use it will remain an object of their attention and, as it is a concept-in-use when teaching is discussed, it must, despite all the semantic problems entailed, remain a component – perhaps even a central component – of educational discourse.

Since the educational issues discussed in this book are contingent upon an acceptance that 'profession' has a generally recognized (if sometimes an elusive as well as an allusive) meaning, its deployment must be justified, and such is the task of the present chapter.

Sociological approaches to the idea of a profession

The debate about the idea of a profession precedes, of course, the attention of sociologists and social historians. However, it is beyond the scope of this book to undertake a detailed historical analysis of the debate about the professions. It was a concept which found a place in the works of the founding fathers of sociology, Weber and Durkheim, but it will be convenient to start at the point where sociologists and other social theorists sought to identify the criteria which distinguished the professions from other occupations; Flexner's (1915) paper is usually taken as marking the beginning of this approach.

The criterion approach essentially entailed inducting a set of distinguishing characteristics and using these as a sort of template against which occupations could be judged in terms of their 'profession-ness'. The term 'inducting' is used here with deliberate intent, since the criteria included in these lists were allegedly not generated by any abstract notion of what a profession *ought* to be like, but were derived ostensibly from an examination of the distinctive characteristics of those occupations which were, by common consent, recognized as professions – medicine, the law, the church, architecture, engineering and the military. These criteria were inducted by noting the

2

presence of such objective factors as the existence of a self-governing body and a written code of ethics. However, this form of interpretation often had an inherent value loading of what a profession *ought* to be. Furthermore, it is obvious that if the criteria were derived from the most prestigious of those occupations generally called professions, those occupations would, of course, meet them. The criteria were self-fulfilling. A thought experiment might well generate different criteria which the alleged professions did not so readily meet. An example of such a criterion might be the continuing professional development of practitioners, which the established professions might not as easily have met as some other occupations at the time when the criteria began to be listed. The established professions are, of course, now much more orientated to practitioner self-development, though they may not meet this criterion to the same degree as others, e.g. teaching.

This 'criterion' approach could never be wholly, 'atheoretical', for the reasons given above, and many formulations were based on an implicit theory which was given its explicit elaboration in the work of Talcott Parsons (1954). This theory was *functionalism*. The basis of this approach was to attribute to the professions certain social functions which were central to the maintenance of the well-being of that social system which we term 'society'. Parsons' writings have an immense subtlety and power, and he did not himself engage in anything as simplistic as drawing up a set of criteria. There *are* criteria, both implicit and explicit, in his work, and the work is infused with value judgement, but Parsons must be exonerated from an over-simplistic approach to the criteria of a profession.

The functionalist argument can be summarized as follows (Hoyle, 1980):

1. A profession is an occupation which performs a crucial social function.
2. The exercise of this function requires a considerable degree of skill.
3. This skill is exercised in situations which are not wholly

3

routine, but in which new problems and situations have to be handled.

4. Thus, although knowledge gained through experience is important, this recipe-type knowledge is insufficient to meet professional demands, and the practitioner has to draw on a body of systematic knowledge.

5. The acquisition of this body of knowledge and the development of specific skills requires a lengthy period of higher education.

6. This period of education and training also involves the process of socialization into professional values.

7. These values tend to centre on the pre-eminence of clients' interests, and to some degree they are made explicit in a code of ethics.

8. Because knowledge-based skills are exercised in non-routine situations, it is essential for the professional to have the freedom to make his own judgements with regard to appropriate practice.

9. Because professional practice is so specialized, the organized profession should have a strong voice in the shaping of relevant public policy, a large degree of control over the exercise of professional responsibilities, and a high degree of autonomy in relation to the state.

10. Lengthy training, responsibility and client-centredness are necessarily rewarded by high prestige and a high level of remuneration. (p. 45)

This schematized argument contains many of the criteria which are alleged to distinguish professions from other occupations. One list of components from the many which have been produced is as follows (Lieberman, 1956):

(a) a unique, definite and essential social service;
(b) an emphasis on intellectual techniques in performing this service;
(c) a long period of specialized training;
(d) a broad range of autonomy for both the individual practitioner and for the occupational group as a whole;
(e) an acceptance by the practitioner of broad personal

responsibilities for judgements made and acts performed
within the scope of professional autonomy;

(f) an emphasis upon the service rendered rather than the
economic gain to practitioners;

(g) a comprehensive self-governing organization of practitioners.
(pp. 2–5)

Although they have heuristic value, such lists reveal some
inherent problems. Apart from the fact already mentioned, that
they have been inducted from the existing high-status professions, it is clear that it is over-simplistic to use such lists to
distinguish between professions and non-professions in a zero-
sum manner. While the high-status professions, by definition,
meet all the alleged criteria in full, many other occupations meet
some but not all the criteria, and those may be met in full or
in part. It is thus possible to conceptualize a continuum, at one
end of which are located the undoubted professions and along
which are ranged occupations which meet only some of the
criteria, and these only in part. These are variously termed the
semi-, quasi- or emergent professions, and, for what it is worth,
teaching is normally held by theorists within this tradition to
be a semi-profession. Presumably there is another end to this
continuum which indicates a cut-off point between the least
profession-like of the professions and those occupations which
are nearly-but-not professions. Such a point is rarely identified,
and can only be achieved with any credibility by means of scal-
ing techniques.

Another inherent problem is that the different occupational
activities of the acknowledged professions make commensur-
ability difficult. The professions are concerned to different
degrees with abstractions, objects, and people, and the same set
of criteria are not wholly relevant to professions as different in
their practices as accountancy, engineering, architecture, law,
medicine, education, and social work. By and large, medicine
has been taken as the paradigm profession, and the character
of its institutions and practices has considerably influenced the
criteria which are most frequently stipulated.

It has been frequently claimed by critics of the criterion approach to the professions that there is a lack of concordance between the various sets which have been produced, and some writers have tabulated these in order to show the degree of commonality, or lack of it (Millerson, 1964). It is certainly the case that there is far from complete consensus among those theorists and researchers who have produced lists. Nevertheless, there remains a high degree of agreement in the case of a small number of criteria – particularly knowledge, autonomy and responsibility – even though there are variations in the inclusion of perhaps less central criteria. Despite this, the criterion approach to the professions, and the functionalist assumptions which frequently underlie it, has been widely criticized. And, since there would appear to be little point in discussing the nature of a profession if there are no agreed criteria by which to define it, the value of using the term profession at all has been questioned in full or in part.

Varieties of criticism of the concept of a profession

Perhaps the most fundamental criticism of the idea of a profession holds that it is less a descriptive than, at best, a symbolic or, at worst, an ideological concept.

The symbolic form has been expressed as follows by Everett C. Hughes (1958), the doyen of the 'Chicago School' of students of occupations and professions. He wrote: 'Profession is a symbol of a man's (*sic*) work and hence of himself' (p. 63). By this is meant that, since the professions have a high status in society, members will seek to sustain or improve their status by having their occupation generally regarded as a profession and hence themselves as professionals. Thus, individuals may seek to create a self-fulfilling prophecy by referring to themselves as professionals and their occupational activities as 'professional'. Moreover, this self-description of an occupation as a profession is one of the key activities of the élites of professional organizations in their interaction with politicians, the media and other influential groups. These efforts to create the recognition of an occupation as a profession are sometimes amusing – especially in the case of those, occupations where professional status is highly dubious – and sometimes a sign of status desperation.

The ideological approach is an extension of the symbolic and denotes a much more political set of activities in which the concept of profession is deployed in a deliberate attempt to influence policy. Studies of this approach emphasize *power* more than *symbol* and attend to the political strategies used by organized occupations to maintain or increase status and the prerequisites which accompany this. In a detailed historical study of the professions in Britain and North America, Larson (1977) has demonstrated how the currently élite professions have been able to create a market for their services, steadily define who is competent to provide these services, achieve a political mandate for the exclusive supply of their services, and enhance their status and power by creating an ideology of professionalism. This perspective on the professions is very different from that of functionalism. In the case of the latter, status is regarded, to put it simplistically, as having been bestowed by a grateful public. In the case of the ideological perspective, status is seen as a function of the power which has accrued to a profession through its increasing control of the market.

The ideological view of the professions differs in its view of the alleged criteria. It sees these less as descriptions of the nature and practice of the professions than as a deliberate attempt at aggrandizement. Thus, the claim to *special knowledge* is held to be greatly exaggerated, in that many of the tasks of the occupations called professions could be equally well carried out by people with less formal education. The academic requirements of professional entrants are seen as a form of credentialism which creates an artificial shortage in qualified personnel. A number of writers have challenged the knowledge claims of the professions, not least in relation to teaching, both from within as well as without the teaching profession. Even the teacher associations have sometimes displayed an ambivalent attitude towards academic knowledge, other than subject content

7

knowledge, recognizing its significance for status but doubting its relevance to practice. However, this ambivalence has been focused on a particular kind of professional knowledge, that which has been codified and systematized according to conventional academic disciplines. As Chapter 3 will indicate, this is a somewhat limited view of professional knowledge. Some radical critics of the alleged knowledge base of the professions have dismissed the claim as a near-total hoax. A more moderate view holds that the knowledge claims for the professions are misguided, in so far as they are predicated upon an application of codified knowledge to professional practice. Some writers (Bennett and Hockenstad, 1973; Haug, 1973) have argued that professional practice in those occupations such as teaching and social work is based more on common sense, intuition and accumulated experience than on a basis of formalized knowledge. And Halmos (1970) has argued that although formalized knowledge may have a minor place, professional practice in what he termed the *personal service professions* was more effectively grounded in a context in which the interpersonal relationship between the professional and the client constituted the essence of what it meant to be a professional.

The criterion of *autonomy* has similarly been the object of much criticism. It has been argued that the claims for practitioner autonomy constitute a defence against the legitimate claim for accountability more than the freedom to do one's best by one's clients. There has been much criticism of the orientation of professionals towards their clients whose problems, in the name of natural or social science, have often been objectified so that the clients themselves are treated in a detached manner, the professional adopting an attitude of, in Parsons' term, *affective neutrality*. This obviously distances the professional from the client and limits the opportunity for the client to engage in a dialogue with practitioners or to call into question their professional practice. At the level of the organized profession there is a widespread criticism that professional bodies deploy institutional means to protect the autonomy of the individual practitioner, against both the individual client – patient, pupil, or parent – and the state as client. It has in recent years been the reaction of the state as client to the perceived protectionism of the professions which has evoked a range of methods for ensuring accountability to all clients – the individual various interest groups, and the state.

Radical critics also call into question the codes of ethics or codes of practice adopted by professional bodies which, in some instances, appear more concerned with protecting practitioners against the legitimate claims for accountability to clients and to control relationships among practitioners themselves rather than to give the edge to clients in the client–practitioner relationship.

The political attack on the professions

The critique of the idea of a profession has a long history among social theorists. George Bernard Shaw, for example, described the professions as 'a conspiracy against the laity'. The apotheosis of this critique was reached in the 1960s and 1970s in the writings of sociologists and social theorists of the political left who were particularly concerned that the power of the professions, supported by a professional ideology, was militating against the interests of individuals and social groups, particularly those who were socially and economically disadvantaged. However, action to curb professional power, and thereby, as a consequence, challenging the professional ideology, came from the political right and was a distinctive feature of Thatcherism.

The Thatcher government took forward with enthusiasm, the accountability movement which had its beginnings under the previous Labour administration, marked by Callaghan's Ruskin Speech of 1976 and the actions of establishing the Taylor Committee on school governors and the Manpower Services Commission. But Thatcherism gave it a distinctive, vigorous ideological thrust. As far as the teaching profession was concerned, the aim was to reverse the trend which led in the 1960s to the high point of professional autonomy at the individual and the collective level, though the movement was not particularly

9

marked by the deployment of 'profession' as a negative concept. None the less, it was a challenge to the freedom of the teacher to decide what should be taught and to the organized professions' influential role in what Manzer (1970) termed the 'sub-government of education'. The organized profession resisted attempts at the central control of curriculum and pedagogy by, for example, limiting David Eccles' attempt to enter 'the secret garden of the curriculum' by resisting his aspirations to establish a curriculum committee in the Ministry of Education to the establishment of a Curriculum Council for England and Wales, the membership of which was numerically dominated by teachers, in effect, representatives of the teacher associations.

The autonomy of the teacher, as defended by the professional associations, was – and still is – held to be responsible for the alleged decline in educational standards by successive conservative governments. It is believed that teachers were encouraged by teacher educators, HMI, LEA inspectors, and a metaphysical entity called 'the educational establishment' to press for multi-disciplinary enquiry, resource-based learning, mixed-ability grouping, and other misguided innovations.

The policies of the successive Conservative governments which have been in power since 1979 have sought to increase the accountability of the professions. This policy was directed at all the professions, even the prestigious professions of medicine and law were not immune. The reorganization of the hospital service, for example, reduced the autonomy of individual doctors to exercise their judgements in relation to patients' needs through increased bureaucratic and financial controls. But it was teaching which experienced the greatest impact.

Thatcherite ideology led to the emergence of two strategies. 'Emergence' is probably the appropriate term here, since thinking was at the ideological and broad policy levels rather than at the level of detail. Actual strategies emerged from a series of tactical choices. The first strategy was that of centralization, which saw the implementation of the National Curriculum and associated testing, a set of policies regarding institutional development plans, teacher appraisal, directed time, the creation of the Council for the Accreditation of Teacher Education, (CATE) etc. The other strategy was the devolution of, particularly financial, responsibilities to the schools and their governing bodies, and the introduction of city technology colleges and grant maintained schools, the purpose of which was partly to undermine the LEAs so that they would fall into desuetude and partly to expose schools and hence teachers to the control of market forces, thereby making them accountable. However, it is also argued by some that this strategy actually increases the autonomy of schools and therefore could be held to be enhancing professional autonomy in education.

The introduction of the CATE criteria for teacher education courses can be conceived as undermining the knowledge base of teaching as a profession. Ministers in Conservative governments have constantly sought to denigrate the role of 'educational theory'. 'Educational theory' – using this term as shorthand for pedagogical theory, curriculum theory, social theory, and the underpinning disciplines of educational psychology, sociology, etc. – was an element in the CATE criteria, though more implicit than explicit. However, government initiatives to shift the site of teacher education from the teacher training institutions to the schools has the deliberate aim of reducing the knowledge base of teaching as a profession.

Current perspectives on the professions with special reference to teaching

The preceding section has briefly illustrated how the idea of a profession has been criticized from an essentially radical left perspective and from the more detached perspective of certain sociological students of the professions. Both groups doubt the continuing value of the concept in social analysis. It also briefly referred to the policies of recent Conservative governments in Britain which in practice, and in vocabulary on occasions, have been concerned with undermining some of those characteristics of a profession which have been held to be their distinguishing characteristics. One must therefore raise the question as to whether 'profession' remains a useful concept in the analysis of social and educational policy. Although many writers claim not, the very title of this book suggests that the present writers believe that, on balance, it is. This position must obviously be justified.

It must first be said that the use of 'profession' as an organizing concept is by no means the only approach to the issues discussed in this book. Questions of knowledge, autonomy and responsibility can be discussed as separate issues or within different theoretical frameworks. For example, Ozga (1988), while concerned with the above as professional issues, chose not to locate her discussion within the conventional framework used for discussing the professions. Her analysis is more influenced by a labour-process approach to teaching and locates the issues identified above within a framework of de-skilling and proletarianization. She writes:

> Among the lines of enquiry which are suggested by looking
> at teaching as work, and considering the meaning of
> professionalism in teachers' work, are those that direct attention
> to the organization of teachers' work and the workplace
> context, to teachers' formal and informal groupings and
> networks, to the division of labour both by function and by
> gender in teaching, to the role of management and supervision,
> to performance appraisal and efficiency, to strategies of
> compliance and resistance, and to job design and quality
> control in education work. . . . In different but related ways the
> recognition of class and gender as central concepts in the study
> of teachers' work lends support to putting professionalism in
> the background and adopting proletarianization as a thesis that,
> at least, merits investigation.'   (p. xii)

From the perspective of this book, de-skilling is clearly an element in de-professionalization and raises no problem. However, proletarianization implies that de-skilling, or de-professionalization, is leading teachers to identify themselves as working class, about which the present writers remain unconvinced.

Despite the problems which it generates, 'profession' has proved to be particularly stubborn in persisting, both as a theoretical concept and as a concept-in-use. It cannot be ignored, and there are a number of ways in which the term might continue to be deployed.

One is purely semantic. An objective approach can be taken to the connotations given to the word 'profession', and related parts of speech, either when used in natural settings or in print or other media, or when construed by particular groups of people (e.g. students,) responding to the word when presented with a stimulus of some kind. The outcome would be some kind of content analysis thereof.

A second is to add to the above methods, or to a somewhat less systematic analysis of usage, an interpretation of the symbolic or ideological intent. Ozga and Lawn (1981), for example, have shown how the teacher associations have deployed the concept of 'profession' in order to attempt to improve status, pay, and conditions, whereas politicians – and they were writing about a period before the Conservative government of 1979 – deployed the term 'profession' to mollify the associations and to seek their acceptance of government policies. Successive Conservative ministers have contrived to deploy the term in this manner and, although no strict content analysis is available to support the view, an impressionistic reading of ministerial statements suggests it is the negative term, 'unprofessional', which is usually applied when militant action is suggested or when there is within the teaching profession widespread dissatisfaction with a particular government policy. That ministers deploy the term 'profession', and related parts of speech in a deliberately political manner is well illustrated by a statement of Kenneth Clarke, though made when he was Secretary of State for Health before he moved to Education. When the ambulance drivers were undertaking militant action on behalf of a pay claim, they deployed the argument that they were professional people and that their professionality deserved financial recognition; Kenneth Clarke replied that they were indeed professional, they were *professional drivers*!

13

A third approach is to undertake research on the extent to which members of an occupation regard themselves as members of a profession. Inevitably, when questionnaires are used, they might be expected to 'lead' respondents towards this idea which they would not otherwise have held, or, at least, consciously held and verbally deployed. No parallel study of teachers has taken Dingwall's (1976) approach towards identifying the concepts used by social workers as they 'accomplish' professionality.

A fourth approach is to eschew the debate about criteria and ideology and to focus upon the occupational practices of members of those occupations normally termed professions. This is the approach which has dominated the 'Chicago School' of occupational sociology, leading members of which are Eliot Freidson (1970), whose studies of medical practice lead the field in this area, and Dan Lortie, whose *Schoolteacher* (Lortie, 1975) is the *locus classicus* in the literature on teaching. This approach to the professions is inductive, and the nature of professionality is garnered from a study of practices and institutions. Freidson is one of those writers who express great reservations about the term 'profession' and would prefer their study to be simply a study of occupations. He recognizes that it would be impossible to dispose of the use of the concept in sociological research and therefore advises a strict operational approach whereby any usage of the term is clearly defined. However, older usages are more persistent than such an approach would allow. If one is studying the practices and institutions of a profession, one is assuming that *a priori* they are professions, which returns one to the problem of criteria.

A fifth approach is to take a historical perspective on the professions. Perkin (1989), for example, has shown how the idea of a profession became a dominant element in the social structure of Britain in the late-nineteenth and early-twentieth century. Having mapped 'the rise of professional society', he ends his study with intimations of its decline or, at least, the decline in the power of the professions which has proceeded apace since he completed his work. As indicated above, Larson's (1977)

14

historical study is more deliberately concerned with 'unmasking' the ideology of professionalism. The two major historical studies of the teaching profession in England and Wales, those of Tropp (1957) and Gosden (1972), have taken, in the case of Tropp, a stance which depicted the teacher associations as pushing forward the professional ideals – while retaining a union strategy – whereas that of Gosden is more general, though illuminated by fascinating detail, namely the rise of teaching as a profession – the concept here being taken for granted.

The approach taken in this book

This book rests within the earlier tradition of the criterion approach. Although many of the objections to the approach are accepted, the idea of a profession, in T.H. Marshall's phrase, 'is not wholly the invention of selfish minds'. Though some of the criteria are perhaps peripheral and others ideological, it does appear that knowledge, autonomy and responsibility remain crucial matters for *education* and can be profitably approached from within the conceptual framework which 'profession' generates, though this approach is one of several. However, while the orientation of this book is, on the whole, positive to the idea of a profession, the term will be used heuristically. It does not merely involve a matching of the educational practice against three of the traditional criteria. It is a question of raising the questions about the *nature* of teacher's autonomy, knowledge, and responsibility, as these relate to effective practice. Thus, although heuristic in that the concept of a profession and three common criteria are used to open up issues of educational practice, values are not wholly absent from the process.

The perspective taken in focusing on professional practice will seek to avoid issues of *status*, what it is, how it is achieved, and how it is sustained. 'Profession', of course, is about status. Occupations which seek to be recognized as professions are hopeful that this will enhance their esteem in the eyes of others, their remuneration, and a range of other perquisites. That can never be discounted. Knowledge, autonomy and responsibility, where the latter is incorporated into a specific code of ethics, are related to status and power, but can be, to a degree, uncoupled from them.

This perspective can be further elaborated by clarifying the terms which are to be used. The term 'profession', can refer to any occupation or to relatively distinctive occupations which, despite problems in achieving total consensus, have distinguishing characteristics on which there is a high degree of consensus, including knowledge base, autonomy, and responsibility. It is this latter definition which, although it is recognized that the term is used both symbolically and ideologically, is adopted as at least a useful heuristic concept. It is further accepted that teaching, though not ranked in status terms with medicine and law, is legitimately the object of this heuristic deployment of the term.

'Professionalization' is generally used to denote the process by which a semi-profession increasingly meets the alleged criteria of a full profession. However, professionalization contains two strands which have been elsewhere distinguished by one of the present writers (Hoyle, 1974). One element is the process of meeting the institutional, and hence status aspects, of a profession: strengthening the boundary, increasing credential requirements, establishing a self-governing body, etc. The other element is improving the quality of the service provided, through improving the skills and knowledge of practitioners. We will use the term 'professionality' to refer to that set of knowledge, skills, values and behaviours which is exercised on behalf of clients. This term is used in preference to the more common 'professionalism' because, although their everyday usage is synonymous, some writers have used 'professionalism' to refer to ideology, rhetoric, and strategies which occupations deploy in the interest of their own self-aggrandizement.

The teaching profession in Britain was, for well over a century, in the process of professionalization as defined above, and its organizations deployed a *professionalism*, also as defined above. A boundary was established between the qualified and unqualified teacher, with the latter eventually disappearing. The same is true of the trained and untrained graduate. The length of the minimum of teacher training increased from two to three, and then, to four years in the single decade of the 1960s, during which time teaching also became an all-graduate profession. The body of academic and professional knowledge increased and was codified through the activity of academics and researchers in institutions of higher education and a range of research and curriculum development bodies. Although there had always been a desire for a General Teaching Council, the profession just failed to achieve this in 1969, and again in 1972 – though the Scottish teachers succeeded. This successful period of professionalization ceased with the accountability movement of the late 1970s, and subsequent pressures from central government have been towards de-professionalization.

Logic suggests that there ought to be a strong relationship between professionalization and increased professionality. However, although this is the orthodox opinion, it cannot be accepted as axiomatic. In the 1980s and early 1990s doubts were increasingly expressed about the professionalization of teachers, particularly the extent to which the length of training had been extended, or even the necessity of having training at all, by politicians and various quasi-political groups. However, the opposite view has been taken in relation to nursing. The relationship between professionalization and professionality must therefore be treated as problematic. We refer to the process by which teachers acquire the knowledge, skills and values which will improve the service they provide to clients as *professional development*, which can be used to embrace initial training, in-service training, and a variety of school-based experiences. The relationship between professional development and professionality is less problematic than that between professionalization and professionality, but the actual relationship is a matter for evaluation studies.

Finally, we come to the most problematic concept of all – 'professional' used as a noun or as an adjective and applied either to a person, an activity, or an attribute. The connotations

17

of this term are so diverse that no purpose would be served by rehearsing these in this context. This is not to underestimate the semantic significance of the use of this term in political or policy debates – as is made clear by Kenneth Clarke's use of the term in relation to the ambulance workers, referred to above – but discussion of specific connotations will occur as appropriate in subsequent chapters.

Conclusion

This book is not directly concerned with status issues entailed in categorizing teaching as a *profession*. The term is taken as a central organizing concept for exploring three aspects of *professionality*: teachers' knowledge, the significance of autonomy for effective practice, and the values and attitudes entailed in the notion of professional responsibility. The term profession is used heuristically. While the writers believe that the idea of a profession continues to present a model towards which occupations should aspire in terms of the professionality of their members, this represents only the broad value context of the book. What is more important is that the term is a starting-point for teasing out some of the complexities of teachers' practices in the three areas identified.

2 Collusion and conflict: teacher–state relations, 1850–1993

Introduction

The modern history of the teaching profession is the history of collusion and conflict between the state and the teacher associations concerning issues of pay and conditions, on the structural aspects of the educational system, and finally on issues of knowledge, autonomy and responsibility. To understand these themes, this chapter will trace both the 'generational dynamics' (Kerchner and Mitchell, 1988) and the complex interrelationship between the characteristics of the teaching profession and its socio-historical framework.

Although essentially a diachronic account of the complex process of change and continuity within an occupational group, the chapter also aims to throw light on the present tensions that prevail within the educational system. To achieve this, the chapter focuses on three interrelated rubrics, all deriving from the pioneering work of Dan Lortie (1975): the organizational, the associational and the professional. The first deals with the role of the teachers within the structural and policy-making framework of the state; the second looks at the teachers' collective response to issues of salary and conditions; the third examines teachers' attempts to promote their status, autonomy and image. Finally, given that the 1980s saw rapid change in relation to all three themes, the period from 1979 to 1993 will be examined separately.

Organizational issues

Since the middle of the last century, teachers have on the whole worked in organizations. The transactions between pupils and teachers have therefore always been mediated by a third party – the state (Lortie, 1975). Deployment of the term is however problematic, and as Grace (1988) points out, it is important to guard against indiscriminate use when discussing the relationship between teachers and their employers. Here, the state should not be seen as a single, uniform entity, but rather as a 'series of agencies, departments, tiers and levels, each with their own rules and resources' (p. 195). Thus the relationship between teachers and this entity we call 'the state' must be seen as operating on various levels (Barber, 1992).

During the early nineteenth century the influence of the state was minimal and education was broadly carried out at local level and responded to local forces. Most of the provision tended to be religious in character and was essentially a mixed economy of Charity, Ragged, Dame and religious schools. The occupational life of the teacher therefore reflected the identity of these schools, and in consequence he or she tended to be a rudimentary deliverer of basic knowledge and skills.

However, as urbanization spread it brought within its wake the growth of multiple-classroom schools. This change in the occupational workplace clearly affected the teacher's role and task. Teachers could no longer be seen as operating individually within an informal setting; instead, this conception was replaced by one of a salaried employee who was becoming increasingly aware of a separate identity. In addition, as schools became more widespread, the pedagogical capacities of teachers became more clearly defined and linked to certification and licensing.

By middle of the nineteenth century, then, the number of children required to attend school had virtually outstripped the supply of teachers, and this problematic relationship between supply and demand was to be a recurring theme throughout the modern history of education. Part of the problem was not only attracting new entrants, but keeping them after qualification. Salary levels were low, conditions of work strenuous, and the temptation to see qualification as a route to better things contributed to low retention rates. Thus the emergence of a skilled, diligent, respected and committed workforce could only develop if the structure, organization and conditions of schooling improved.

This 'organizational imperative', as Lortie (1975) calls it, was therefore crucial to the future emergence of teachers as an organized occupational group, and an analysis of the relationship between teachers and the state in terms of the policy-making framework is vital to our overall understanding of the teaching profession.

During the quarter of a century following the end of the Second World War, teachers played a major role in policy-making, a factor that was associated with what has been called the 'Butskellite consensus'. Although with hindsight a great deal of this convergence can be seen as more procedural than substantive, the collective voice of teachers was heard within the corridors of power. This apparent influence of teachers in the decision-making process was associated with the rise in workplace autonomy and the close relationship established with the new organs of curricular and pedagogical influence.

One of the major structural issues facing both the state and teachers at this time was the organization of the school system. The 1944 Act enshrined the concept of tri-partitism (although in practice this usually meant continued bi-partitism), while the Labour Party's conversion to the policy of comprehensivization, and the teachers' broad support for such moves, sparked a vigorous debate about the relative value and validity of the 11+ examination and the status of the grammar schools. Much of the debate was fought out within the confines of the educational press, but some spilled over into the pubic domain (Lowe, 1988). The eventual issue of Circular 10/65, and the reorganization that followed, despite resistance in some quarters, was eventually successful, and within a decade nearly 90 per cent of state schools had been transformed. The collusion of teachers with the state over this reform, although not uniform, did represent a triumph of both internal initiation within the profession and external transaction outside (Archer, 1982).

The influential role played by teachers and the levels of co-operation with the state during the period of partnership in educational policy and practice in the post-1944 era stands in direct contrast to the decades preceding the outbreak of war in 1914. Here teachers were limited to a minor role in the significant organizational changes that emerged during the latter quarter of the nineteenth century.

In this phase, the relative newness of teaching as an organized occupation, combined with the multiple goals of the state and other influential groups, created a situation in which teachers reacted to, rather than initiated, organizational change. Musgrave (1970) argues that the various groups who had an interest in structural change in education created a tension which allowed the system to evolve incrementally, and for policy to be defined and redefined. In practice, this meant that change occurred organically within the education system, and although teachers were marginalized from playing a central role in the growth of organized schooling during the years up to 1914, their actions did mean that eventually their influence would have an effect.

This period was marked by three major pieces of legislation: the Revised Code of 1861, and the Education Acts of 1870 and 1902; all of which heralded significant changes that were to have long-term effects. The first is a prime example of the ways in which organizational changes were developing without recourse to teachers, and provides an interesting parallel with later, more contemporary developments.

The Code was imposed by a government concerned about the levels of literacy and numeracy throughout the country. The legislation was therefore driven by an apparent widespread dissatisfaction with the performance of teachers, who were regarded by many as dangerous social climbers who neglected the majority of their pupils in their selfish quest for higher social status. This, combined with the needs of a rapidly industrializing economy and increased overseas competition, saw education become the engine which would drive home Britain's technological advantage.

The Code also revealed a deeper and more sinister intention to control teachers and teaching by introducing a rigid system of reward and punishment for the delivery of a prescribed curriculum. In effect, it put teachers at the mercy of local managers who could make or break careers according to the results. As Hansard noted on 25 March 1861, 'another advantage of the new system is that it gives managers almost unfettered freedom in regulating their schools as they please . . .'

The legislation, then, was a direct attack on the fledgeling autonomy and fragile status of teachers, but it simultaneously gave them the incentive to organize and defend themselves collectively. The concerted attack on the legislation which emerged over the next decade therefore played a major role in cementing their early solidarity: marches were organized, petitions gathered, letters sent and articles written; this well-orchestrated pressure was indicative of the rising sense of collective consciousness among the teachers as a separate occupational group.

The 1870 Act further extended the state's role in education by setting up and funding local school boards which were to locally control educational organizations. These were the precursors of the modern Local Education Authorities (LEAs) which were to be such a central part of the 1902 Act. These school boards eventually became the local state intermediaries, and, according to Grace (1988) 'although often themselves in a fluid, dynamic and sometimes tense relationship with central government, they did represent a major influence on the sort of rapport the teachers' groups sought to establish with their employers'.

The 1902 Act, on the other hand, highlighted the relative weakness of the teachers in relation to their ability to influence national legislation. The Act further developed the provisions of 1870 and placed the control of existing schools and the development of secondary education in the hands of the newly formed LEAs. Thus, by confirming a commitment to, and by

23

encouraging these new authorities to create secondary schools on top of the elementary system, the state was further delineating the teacher's role and simultaneously creating a demarcation between the phases. It was hoped that the new secondary-school graduates would provide most of the recruits for the elementary schools; while the most able secondary-school pupils would proceed to higher education and then perhaps be recruited to the middle-class grammar and private schools.

The teachers were ambivalent in their attitude towards the changes. On the one hand they bemoaned their loss of influence on local education policy-making through the demise of the old school boards, but were at the same time positive about the attempt to elongate the route into teaching by requiring attendance at a secondary school.

Grace (1988) has referred to this two-pronged attack on the teachers as part of a strategy of 'cross-cultural transformation' whereby the state was able to distance the teachers from direct political involvement through the LEAs while at the same time strengthening the secondary sector at the expense of the elementary, thereby catching teachers in their own status trap.

The inter-war period saw further changes in the teachers' role in influencing policy-making, reflecting Lortie's (1975) dictum that teachers were 'Special but Shadowed'. Much of the dynamic of this trend grew out of the increased professionalism engendered by the spread of elementary and secondary education, and in a concomitant rise in collective unity. The 1918 Fisher Act was supported, as were the Hadow Report of 1928 and the Spens Report a decade later. In addition, the abandonment in 1926 of the Board of Education's attempt to control more closely the content of the curriculum, was seen by teachers as a further endorsement of their power and professional status.

Despite the emergence of significant levels of agreement between government and the teachers in relation to this legislative and organizational framework, the further strengthening of state power was always a barrier to complete unity. In fact, the gradual shift in terminology from the Board of Education in the 1920s and 1930s to the Ministry of Education in the post-war decades, to the Department of Education and Science in the 1970s, and eventually to the Department for Education in the 1990s, was indicative of the growing power and importance of the polity and bureaucracy in policy-making and administration. The power of the state to control the organizational framework was perhaps underestimated by teachers during the period of relative harmony up to the mid-1970s, a position that has been reflected in the changing relationship over the past fifteen years.

The post-1975 period has been characterized by a willingness of central government increasingly to dictate the direction of policy without recourse to those who work within it. The 1988 Act and the imposition of the National Curriculum were both instigated without the consent or consultation of the educational professionals, and the increased marginalization of teachers from power has been mirrored by the incorporation of all organizational decision-making into the orbit of state policy.

Professional issues

Although such diverse occupations as teachers, footballers and nurses are often referred to as professional, none can claim to be truly professional in the sense of the term as it is applied to medicine. One of the major factors inhibiting the teacher's search for professional status is the very nature of their employment contract: they do not enjoy the independence of the lawyers or medics through the power of client relationship, and instead have to work for a virtual monopolistic employer – the state – which still purchases their services through a delegated relationship with Local Education Authorities (Gosden, 1972). In this way, successive governments have always been able to exert control over both training and recruitment. Teachers, on the other hand, have been unable to regulate entry to their ranks, and simultaneously unable to judge what counts as professional conduct. Both these functions belong firmly to the state and its surrogate organs.

Nevertheless, as a result of prolonged effort, British teachers

25

have been able to negotiate some level of professional autonomy; so much so, that they have until recently enjoyed a workplace independence that was the envy of their European
counterparts. Moves to gain this autonomy have been ham-
pered historically by the determination of the state to maintain
control over the teaching workforce and by inherent segmenta-
tion within the profession.

The story of the teachers' struggle to overcome this segmenta-
tion and to increase their independence and status is best
characterized in the struggle to form a Teachers' Council at the
beginning of the century, and by attempts to increase control
over the supply, training and recruitment of personnel.

It was in the 1840s, under the stewardship of James Kay Shut-
tleworth, that these two issues were first addressed. He realized
that such problems could only be understood and solved by
state intervention, and therefore devised the teacher–pupil
system of training. Thus after completing five years' continuous
service the teacher–pupil could enter a competitive examination
for entrance to a teachers' college and automatically become
eligible for a grant and protected pension rights. By 1850, then,
the state had begun its role as gatekeeper to the profession, a
role it was to strengthen throughout the period under review.
The teachers, it seems, were generally supportive of these moves
and viewed them as part of the state's recognition of their value
and worth. However, in retrospect they were to remain a major
stumbling-block in moves towards professional acceptance.

Despite the gradual drift towards certification and the feeling
of some form of professional unity through the culture of the
training colleges, the middle decades of the nineteenth century
were still marked by a number of tensions between the state and
the teachers. These centred on general levels of dissatisfaction
with both salaries and the occupational status accorded to
elementary school teachers.

Throughout the last quarter of the nineteenth century, the
social status and position of elementary school teachers was a
thorny issue. Many felt themselves to be inferior to the secondary teacher, both in terms of education and salary, and a major

objective of the teachers was to change this position even if it meant breaking any relative harmony between them and the state. The late Victorian chattering classes were often openly hostile to teachers, and their public image suffered from a mixture of public fear and private prejudice.

Furthermore, the position taken by Robert Morant, the Secretary to the Board of Education, in his envisaged changes to the training, certification and recruitment of teachers was, as Grace (1987) suggests, 'a response to the activity and aspirations of elementary school teachers' (p. 200). A crucial element in this policy of 1904 was the increased control by the Board of Education over entry to training colleges. Teachers were therefore placed in a quandary: on the one hand they were still sentimentally committed to the old teacher–pupil system, feeling, somewhat strangely, that the new colleges would not be as effective in producing good-quality teachers as the training schools (Tropp, 1970). On the other hand, the colleges, with their prestige and controlled entry, did go part of the way to conferring higher status on the occupation, and were seen by many as being a major step on the road to full professional recognition.

In conjunction with this, a number of other tensions were emerging: first, could the National Union of Teachers and the Board of Education ensure a balance between supply and demand? The constant fear of over-supply hung like a spectre over the union in its early days. Second, the union wanted assurances that weak but nevertheless highly qualified teachers were weeded out before gaining bursaries, while at the same time pressing for the need for a highly qualified workforce.

So although operating on a different agenda from the state, organized teachers saw the logic in accepting the transformation of recruitment and training, while at the same time pressing for more control over it. This has been a recurrent professional dilemma for generations of teachers – for the structural reforms begun in 1902 allowed the state increasingly to take control over this area, yet, as Grace (1987) points out, with each of these changes, the teachers saw something that appealed to their self-interest, so although discontented, no real crisis emerged.

The continued campaign for a Teachers' Register was also a part of this process. The Register, when it arrived in 1907, did not live up to expectations. It was divided into two groups (columns A and B) relating to certificated (mainly elementary) and secondary teachers. This policy of apartheid grouped teachers on both educational and social grounds and reflected the prejudices and condescension (Grace, 1987) displayed by the Board and its secretary, Robert Morant.

The perversion of the Register (Tropp, 1957) provoked bitter hostility and resistance. The 'caste' nature of the categories was further aggravated by the refusal of the Treasury to allow any money to be spent other than the income raised by the registration fees. For four years the Register staggered to its fateful end under bitter attacks from both the NUT and from constant underfunding by the Board of Education. In 1907 it announced it could not successfully carry out its duties under the present conditions and the Board took the opportunity to abolish it. This move provoked further hostility from the union, and the Board was forced to reconstitute the Register. For three more years the representatives of the various interest groups continued to meet to thrash out a solution. This was achieved by an Order of the Council in 1912.

However, it was doomed to fail. The tension and dissatisfaction engendered by the government's attitude in general, and Morant's attitude in particular, was brought to a head in the infamous Holmes-Morant Circular affair of 1911. In the document, elementary teachers were described variously as 'uncultured, imperfectly educated' and characterized as 'creatures of routine'. This led the authors of the circular to conclude that 'LEAs should, wherever possible, try to replace them with university educated teachers.' The NUT reacted with ferocity, and through the power of their lobby were able to force the resignation of Morant. As Grace (1987) points out, the events of 1911 were the most 'dramatic manifestation of the NUT's capacity to mobilise political power against the agency of the State in Education' (p. 202).

The campaign also highlighted both the strengths and weaknesses of organized teachers. In terms of the former, governments were forced to take notice of their collective power and realized that high-handedness could provoke a dangerous reaction. The event also showed up several weaknesses: first, the notion of 'Victorian exclusiveness' still reigned and the gulf between secondary and elementary teachers remained. Second, the state, having become a force in education, now had a vested interest in opposing any move towards a Teachers' Register, and the history of the next four decades illustrates the validity of this claim.

Despite being shadowed, the 1920s did see teachers gain further curricular autonomy. Fears of a centralized and perhaps socialist appropriation of the curriculum led the Board of Education further to relax its controls over the curriculum in 1926; and in moving from 'prescription to suggestion', claims Ozga (1992), 'the state were (sic) laying the foundations of a policy of curriculum autonomy which was to last until the mid-1980s'.

This version of 'responsible autonomy' was to be the hallmark of teacher–state relations for the next half century. In this sense teachers were promoted by the state to meet the requirements of the state but were given a measure of workplace independence and room for manoeuvre in the classroom. This form of organizational control required the government to construct a model of a teacher who was non-political, being concerned solely with the education of the young, who had a vocational calling, who used accepted pedagogical methods, who was morally responsible and, above all, safe.

That the teachers broadly acquiesced in this characterization is important for our understanding of the levels of collusion and conflict between teachers and the state. Clearly, the leaders of the teachers' organizations believed that such an approach was part of the drift towards professionalism and also helped to safeguard the unions from further divisions. The state, on the other hand, could rightfully claim that they were pursuing their political objectives without due interference from militant

29

action, as well as stressing the importance of partnership between the teachers, and both central and local government. Kerchner and Mitchell (1988) have argued that one of the essential elements in this generation of teacher–state relations is the apparent subordination of industrial action to professional issues and the needs of the client. In this sense both the state and the teachers could therefore claim that they were keeping industrial strife from interfering with the education of children.

Despite being heralded as an era of partnership, the post-war period was marked by a fluctuating tension between what Attlee called the teachers' 'spiritual and intellectual' calling and the more hard-nosed traditional trade-union issues of salary maintenance and conditions of service. For the state, on the other hand, the immediate post-war optimism and the desire for co-operation and planning saw teachers exalted as key personnel in the creation of the New Jerusalem. This belief in collaboration and the widespread acceptance of the 1944 Act became the basis of the settlement. Despite the special role of teachers in this conception, they still had to struggle to maintain both parity of salary and public esteem. By 1950 the optimistic shine was beginning to wear off as cracks began to appear in the consensus: public expenditure constraints and the need to improve the supply of teachers clashed; in the six years since the passing of the Act teachers' salaries declined, and by 1950 *The Times* admitted that 'teachers needed to be uplifted in terms of their monetary reward' (Cunningham, 1992, p. 38).

Furthermore, the 1960s also saw teachers play an increased role in the organizational changes taking place in relation to pedagogy and the curriculum. The Plowden Report of 1965, gave credence to a new form of child-centred primary school teaching, and the rise of comprehensivization saw teachers begin to play formative roles in the construction of a variety of new curricula. Many of these developments were supported by the teachers' associations, and the creation of the Schools Council, for instance, saw teacher involvement in curriculum and pedagogical reform reach its apogee. Thus, by the beginning of the 1970s teachers were able to exert a degree of control over the curriculum of which their forefathers, a century ago, would have been both envious and proud.

This enhanced curriculum authority and the continued development of greater workplace autonomy not only compensated for the relative decline in the value of teachers' salaries, but appeared to be indicative of the gradual move to increased professional status. However, in their quest for greater overall professional control, particularly in terms of training, selection and certification, teachers still lagged way behind the established professions. Nevertheless, they could console themselves with the thought that increased university involvement and the compulsory nature of training would eventually lead to improved status and the emergence of some kind of controlling professional body.

Associational issues

According to Lortie (1975) the 'Associative factor' is crucial to any understanding of the changing relationship between the state and the teachers. The advent of large-scale elementary education for the poor and the rise of industrialization in the nineteenth century saw schools being constructed in communities which reflected the new dynamics in society. The rise of the teachers' associations, like the development of trade unionism in general, mirrored these changes, and although never really suffering from the geographical fragmentation which characterized many other craft unions, early teacher associations did suffer from the perennial problem of differential pay and conditions (Barber, 1992).

Associational life took on a new meaning after 1870 with the setting up of the National Union of Elementary Teachers, an organization that was 'conceived in protest and grew in an atmosphere of conflict' (Tropp, 1957). From its inception its primary aims were to further the broad professional status of teachers, to be a forum for debate, and if necessary to be a vehicle for action. Its medium-term objectives related therefore to exerting greater control and authority over entry by campaigning for a teachers' professional register; to improving promotion and career prospects, particularly by opening up the inspectorate to more teachers; and finally to establishing and maintaining a comprehensive pension package for its members.

By concentrating on these 'bread and butter' issues, the National Union of Teachers (as it was now called) was able to achieve considerable success. By the turn of the century, for instance, security of employment was strengthened, teacher involvement in the inspectorate was increased (although it still remained woefully inadequate), and negotiations, albeit controversial, had begun concerning the setting up of a Teachers' Registration Council.

In terms of the generational dynamics of teacher–state relations, the first decade of the twentieth century can be seen as a period of growing unease associated with the ending of the first harmonious generation and the birth of the second. Discontent, according to Kerchner and Mitchell (1988), usually flows from flaws within the existing system when new ideas are introduced despite opposition, thus setting the stage for conflict and crisis.

As well as the problems and controversies surrounding the Register, a variety of other associational issues were giving concern. In the years preceding the First World War a bottle-neck in terms of promotion and career advancement had occurred. Ozga and Lawn (1981) have shown that teachers, particularly in London, were continually fighting a combination of controls and duties forced on them by their employers. This was aggravated by the longstanding problem of salary levels and conditions of service. In 1896 the NUT was involved in its first major industrial conflict when it reacted against a local school board's decision to sack four teachers who ignored an early attendance rule. Similarly, in West Ham in 1907, a dispute arose after a new LEA alliance of ratepayers tried to force down teachers' salaries. Despite blackleg labour, the NUT was able to mobilize local support and force a favourable settlement. Barber (1992) claims that such events signified the union's readiness to move

32

beyond meet-and-confer status, and to engage in more confrontational bargaining positions.

These disputes, and others of the pre-war and war years, must also be seen within the general framework of the increased militancy that swept across the industrial landscape of Britain during the Edwardian period. In 1913 the union set up a special salaries committee to organize a national campaign to counter the fall in living standards which had been evident since the start of the previous year. At local level the union was still involved in a protracted attempt to gain union recognition in small isolated rural areas. This was typified by the longest strike in British history, at Burston's School, which began on 1 April 1914 and lasted until 1939.

Although suspending immediate action on the outbreak of war in the summer of 1914, the campaign was renewed two years later as teachers' salaries once again fell behind prices. This, combined with more stringent entry regulations, made it more difficult for new working-class novices to enter the profession. Also, the war years saw an overall increase in class size and a lengthening of the school day, moves that further hindered adequate recruitment. The rise of militancy by the teachers alarmed the government, who were still reeling under the seismic effects of the recent revolution in Russia and the genuine fear of further class conflagrations at home. By the end of the war the new Secretary of the Board of Education, H. A. L. Fisher, had begun to see the dangers of further enraging a group who could play such a significant role in radicalizing the young. As a result Fisher was instrumental in setting up a departmental committee to inquire into the principles which should determine the salary scales of teachers.

This emerged on top of the threat of strike action and followed on from a series of local disputes which underscored rising levels of regional and grassroots militancy. None was more evident than in the Rhondda teachers' strike of 1919. Led by two young activists, W. G. Cove and Gwen Ray, the movement sent shock waves through the union and government alike. The strike quickly gained local and national support and

33

catapulted Cove on to a national stage. The strike was also significant because it showed elements of rising class consciousness within the NUT, particularly in the attempt to forge links with other groups of the organized working class (Lawn, 1987).

Both Cove and Ray were members of the Plebs League, and their actions, it seems, were very much influenced by the syndicalist tradition of the South Wales working-class movement. However, despite its importance to the mythology of the teachers' movement, there are a number of points that need to be made regarding its significance. First, as an event it was rooted in the culture and politics of South Wales and it received support from the almost institutionalized South Wales Miners' Federation, or 'The Fed' as it was known; second, recent research into the action of local grassroots members in the conservative and rural area of Sussex paints a contrasting picture of extreme calm and moderation. Here, the politicization of the union was resisted, and even the call to support women's suffrage was hailed as an unnecessary interference in the solely professional union. Even the strike at Burston's School did not warrant a mention in the minutes of local branch meetings (Griggs, 1991).

Nevertheless, both the symbolic and real fears presented by the teachers did result in the Burnham Committee offering the teachers a generous non-contributory pension scheme and a more wide-ranging salary structure with a built-in career path. The state had therefore realized that confronting the teachers at such a difficult political and economic juncture was too dangerous, and instead was willing to grant teachers some of the trappings of professionalism, in this case limited workplace autonomy combined with a civil-service type career framework.

The following four years were, however, marked by tension. The changing economic climate and the ending of the postwar boom effectively finished the *rapprochement* between the teachers and the state, as many of the early gains were reneged upon in the face of the growing economic depression. The 1921 salary cuts of 5 per cent recommended by the Geddes Committee were resisted and the government was forced to abandon the move. In addition, in July 1922, a Select Committee tried to backtrack on an earlier commitment to the non-contributory pension scheme and called for a 5 per cent contribution from the teachers. Despite seeing this as a betrayal (Barber, 1992), teachers were forced to accept the *fait accompli* issued by the government.

The inter-war decades were characterized by violent economic and political swings. The aetiology of the period is complex and involves a concatenation of local, national and international events. The central industrial event of the 1920s was the General Strike, and although class antagonisms hardened, the teachers broadly remained on the government's side of the barricades. However, the failure of the strike set in motion a period of industrial relations that were to have profound repercussions for the teachers and other unions.

The need to rein in public expenditure, a persistent theme in educational policy-making, was a high priority for all governments during the period. The teachers therefore had to contend with continued attempts to reduce their salary levels, a situation which created an undercurrent of militancy. This was augmented by a rising tide of activism as the effects of the Depression began to bite, a process that led many in the union to follow a leftward path. Such conditions led the state into a series of dilemmas. Following Grace (1988), these dilemmas can be reformulated as three interlocking questions:

1. To what extent could the state fulfil its objective of reducing public expenditure without provoking a hostile and militant reaction from teachers?

2. What level of classroom autonomy could the state permit without handing over complete control to the teachers during a period of intense politicization?

3. Should the teachers be treated as a non-political profession, and therefore be regarded as trustworthy?

In order to navigate their way around these questions Lawn and Ozga (1986) suggest that the Secretary of the Board of Education, Sir Eustace Percy, practised a policy of 'indirect rule'; a strategy that had been successfully used in Britain's colonial administration. It implied that rather than exercising direct control over teachers and incapacitating them with oaths of loyalty, as many MPs and much of the press were demanding, it would be more sensible to use a more subtle method of control, namely a policy of licensed professionalism (Dale, 1981).

Thus, by playing on the teachers' apparent desire for professional status, Percy carefully operated a strategy of 'trusting the teachers' whereby they were to be given classroom autonomy, a new Burnham salary scale, and improved promotion prospects. This, combined with the effects of the economic downturn, saw teaching become increasingly attractive to university graduates and those of varying social rank. This embourgeoisement of the profession clearly had an effect on the professional image of teachers, which, despite some press hostility, on the whole remained high in public estimation.

The state was aided in its approach by the splits and internal wranglings within the NUT. The first major dissension occurred over its position on equal pay. The adoption in 1919 of such a policy resulted in a succession of male and female members forming separate unions. The former group left in protest and formed the National Association of Male Teachers (which was later to become the National Association of Schoolmasters), while the latter broke away to form the National Union of Women Teachers (these eventually rejoined the NUT when equal pay was established in 1946).

The second major internal issue was that of political affiliation. A referendum on the question of Labour Party membership was defeated by 29,743 to 15,434 votes. The narrowness of the vote was a surprise, and showed that further discussion of the issue could not be postponed indefinitely. On the fringes of the movement many members joined the left-wing Teachers' Labour League in 1923, an organization that tried to forge links with the wider international labour movement and called for the ending of capitalist indoctrination in the classroom.

Perkin (1989) has argued that professionals played a crucial role in the post-1945 world and increasingly came to be seen as the arbiters of the modern welfare state. However, he has identified the late 1960s as the point at which the consensus underpinning the era of social democracy began to crack, and notes that in the months before the general election of 1970 the apparently symbiotic relationship between teachers and the state finally broke down.

The 1950s had seen a dispute over the debts accruing to the teachers through their pension, but although national action was threatened, the dispute was settled amicably. Also, the Durham LEA's attempt to impose a closed shop, despite having advantages for the NUT, was opposed on the grounds of choice, a factor that points to the continued ideology of professionalism within the ranks of the union.

By the end of the 1960s, however, cracks had begun to appear in this professional partnership as dissatisfaction with remuneration and frustration with the career log-jam began to gather pace. This was accompanied by various populist and academic attacks on the apparently low standards of education, thereby heralding a period of discontent and crisis. Likewise, the teacher unions were becoming increasingly militant as the decline in real wages and the lack of promotion posts began to bite. The acrimonious strike action of 1970 illustrated these tensions and brought a swift response from both the press and government, so much so that the militancy of teachers, exemplified in the call for strike action, made the front page in *The Times*.

So, in the closing months of 1969, the consensus that had apparently governed the education service for almost five decades broke down. And as the decade ended, the terms accountability, standards and militancy were beginning to reverberate around the corridors of the educational establishment.

Professionals under siege, 1975-93

The 1970s

The early 1970s marked the beginning of the end of the post-war period of partnership in the educational service, and the closing years of the decade saw the introduction of a new set of relationships which were to be characterized by a power struggle over:

1. The levels of control and autonomy exercised over the curriculum by the state.

2. The levels of accountability to which teachers were increasingly required to succumb.

3. The levels of resources that were to be committed to the educational sector in a time of economic contraction.

The result of the interaction of these three tensions saw teacher–state relations move on to a new plane, to the extent that many of the old certainties and most of the previous strategies were to prove inadequate against a series of radical Conservative governments intent on breaking the mould of British politics.

The decade was ushered in with a bitter pay dispute in which increasingly hostile positions made a mockery of the era of so-called consensus. In fact, the late 1960s had seen education become the site of increasing ideological conflict, with the efficacy of the system coming under pressure from the political left and right. In terms of the former, both Anthony Crosland and A.H. Halsey were beginning to doubt the grand claims that had been made about the ability of a comprehensive system to improve opportunity and increase equality. While on the right, critics believed that traditional values and learning were being undermined and increasingly pupils were leaving school ill-equipped to service the needs of industry. The Black Papers of 1969 and the *cause célèbre* of the William Tyndale School appeared to symbolize the decline of formal education.

Such concerns were brought further into the limelight with successive governments' attempts to control the levels of public expenditure. The use of rate capping, for instance, led to growing tensions between central and local government over levels of resourcing and control. But despite tight budgetary measures, the state's attempts to influence the curriculum, pedagogy and assessment still proved problematic.

The 1976 Ruskin College Speech by the Labour Prime Minister James Callaghan, however, marks a watershed in the state's attempt to overcome resistance to intervention in what was still regarded as the 'Secret Garden' of the curriculum. The text made it clear that the Indian summer (Barber, 1992) of collusion between the state and teachers was over, and that increasingly the educational system and those who worked within it would have to succumb to the needs of a national economic agenda. The Great Debate that followed saw the state begin to exert increasing central control over the curriculum and assessment – a process begun with the issuing of Circular 14/77, which required LEAs to develop tighter and more coherent curriculum policies.

The decade also saw a widespread contraction in employment, and increasingly concerns about the quality of learning were being linked to the competency of teachers, a process that was to lead to further attacks on their workplace autonomy. Throughout the century, despite increasingly falling behind in terms of monetary rewards, teachers could always point to the high level of classroom autonomy as one of the salient characteristics of the job. In defending this position teachers continually pointed to their historic role as valued partners in the educational enterprise whose professional judgement, expertise, knowledge and skills were of central importance to the educational system. Such a defence was to prove flimsy when confronted by the concepts of rational managerialism and curriculum accountability, backed by direct legislative intervention.

1979–93

For many, 1979 was a political, social and economic watershed; a turning-point which ushered in a new set of values that overturned the liberal consensus of previous decades. According to this interpretation, Thatcherism brought in its wake new social and economic relationships characterized by the cash nexus and the fundamentals of the market-place. Others have derided the revolutionary implications implicit in this description and have instead pointed to the evolutionary elements in Thatcherism. In this alternative conception, the changes of the 1980s are seen as an intensification of previously constructed policies. Here commentators point to the importance of accountability, the control of public expenditure and economic restructuring as recurring themes across the decades. Whatever view is taken, an understanding of the phenomenon of Thatcherism is essential to the history of the changing relationship between teachers and state.

Even in the 1990s, the term Thatcherism is destined to remain synonymous with the politics of the New Right. However, to see it as a uniform brand of consistent policies would be a gross over-simplification. In reality, Thatcherism was, and still is, an umbrella term for numerous contradictory ideological influences. It was and remains part of a neo-liberal thread associated with the *laissez-faire* economics of such diverse characters as Adam Smith, Frederick von Hayek and Milton Friedman, while at the same time embracing traditional conservative authoritarianism with its belief in the restoration of so-called traditional values and hierarchical social structures epitomized by the primacy of the nation state. These contradictory and paradoxical elements managed to cohere and coagulate into 'popular authoritarianism' (Hall and Jaques, 1983). This notion became the focus for a number of satellite organizations that sprung up around the government, all with semi-official titles, for instance, the Centre for Policy Studies, the Adam Smith Institute, and the Campaign for Real Education. All, in effect, continued the fight begun by the Black Papers of 1969.

A central element of their ideology was the attack on the manufactured liberal consensus of the post-war world, in which successive Conservative and Labour governments had colluded to produce agreement on a variety of social, political and economic issues; the educational establishment thus became a pejorative term, and its destruction the main thrust of policy. In addition, Thatcherism was also concerned with the re-establishment of market forces as the dynamic behind economic and social change. In education this effectively meant the application of greater choice in terms of parent power and the imposition of an internal market within the maintained sector of schooling.

This combination of populism, decentralization and increased state power, although paradoxical, was a powerful cocktail, in the face of which teachers' traditional strategy of collective bargaining and rational negotiation were a poor match. So although associational issues were to dominate the early and middle years of the decade, it was in the organizational and policy-making field that Thatcherism was to have its greatest impact.

The protracted struggle of the teachers' unions in terms of salary and conditions between 1985 and 1987 marked the high point of their opposition to the government. Although essentially a pay dispute, the conflict was as much about the future direction of the profession as it was about salary levels. The eventual acceptance of Kenneth Baker's pay spine under the Teacher's Pay and Conditions Act, and the imposition of directed time as laid down by the government, marked the beginning of the end of the fight over autonomy and control which had been raging intermittently since the imposition of the Revised Code more than a century before.

The ending of the dispute also paved the way for the Great Education Reform Bill of 1988, an Act that was to effectively undo the structures created in 1944. The Bill, however, had been preceded by numerous other pieces of legislation, all of which contained the essential paradoxes of Thatcherism: greater state control combined with increased market flexibility, manifested in the icon of parental choice. Despite opposing many of the changes, the teachers were unable to resist the juggernaut of state power backed by the inevitability of substantial House of Commons majorities.

So the increased control over the curriculum outlined in the

41

1988 Act, the greater surveillance of teachers' work through the rise of managerialism, the decoupling of teachers from their professional and advisory power bases in LEAs, and the rise of appraisal, examination league tables, and performance-related pay, led teachers to feel truly under siege.

Conclusions

The last decade and a half has seen the education system undergo a radical transformation, particularly in terms of administration and policy; whether such changes have brought about a revolution in attitudes is a different matter. Control over the teaching profession has become more overt, a process helped by the rise of managerialism as a significant force at school level. Here heads and deputies have become the hierarchical agents of both control and implementation, and therefore crucial to the process of accountability. However, such authority has been bought at a price, and the resolution of the tensions between managers and teachers may well prove to be the litmus test by which professional attitudes can be deemed to have changed.

In addition, the period has been marked by the ending of the informal but nevertheless powerful tri-partite arrangement between the DES (DFE), the LEAs and the teachers' associations. Thus the state is now able to exercise power through its network of quangos, of which the Schools' Curriculum and Assessment Authority and the planned Teacher Training Agency are the most recent manifestations. Furthermore, this control is augmented through the operation of market forces in the shape of Local Management of Schools, Grant Maintained Status, the publication of examination league tables, the enhancement of school budgets according to their popularity, and more recently in the attempt to encourage the setting up of new 'specialist' schools with supported state funding.

These movements have been underpinned not only by an overt ideology, but also by a period of financial austerity, and here the marginal effects of the ephemeral mid-1980s boom did very little to stall the onward march of economic contraction. Such changes clearly brought the remuneration question to the forefront, and the decade was dominated by one of the longest and most protracted industrial disputes.

For teachers, the period has also been marked by a crisis of self-confidence and a lowering of public esteem. This has been most noticeable in the media, where teachers' professional image has been put under the microscope on numerous occasions. And yet 1993 and 1994 have seen some modest victories for those core values, in particular the government's climbdown over Key Stage three assessments, the emergence of the Dearing Review and the ending of the 'Mums' Army' fiasco. However, the associational, organizational and professional reforms put in place during the last parliamentary session are well-bedded, so much so that reform and repeal are unlikely well into the next millennium. Nevertheless, teachers have a long history of adaption, and for well over a century have alternately resisted and colluded with the state according to the pragmatic demands of the time. Of crucial importance over the next decade will be their continued attempts to re-establish new forms of autonomy and control through collaborative measures at intra-school and inter-school level. So despite suffering serious setbacks, the teachers' march towards professional status continues, and the omnipresence of the term in every staffroom illustrates their determination to maintain not only their self-concept, but also their belief in the power and efficacy of their own judgement.

3 The issue of professional knowledge

Introduction

Investigating the concept of professional knowledge as it applies to teaching is a complex task. Problems arise not only from the contestability of the construct, but also from the wide variety of theoretical models that have been used to explain and describe it. In 1978, for instance, N.L. Gage, a leading advocate of the teaching effectiveness paradigm, claimed that teaching should be based upon scientific knowledge and felt that 'good teaching' would soon be 'attainable by closely following rigorous laws that yield high predicability and control' (p. 17). In a similar vein, W.E. Gardner, in the preface to a recently edited compendium of papers entitled *Knowledge Base for the Beginning Teacher* (Reynolds, 1989), wrote of the need for teaching to be defined more closely by a codified body of professional knowledge and claimed that the purpose of the book was to 'demonstrate that teaching does have a distinctive knowledge base, that the knowledge is expressed in articulated understandings, skills and judgements which are professional in character' (p. lx).

Many of the claims made on behalf of this group have rested on a rationalist conception of knowledge, based on traditional scientist claims to validity and reliability. However, from a more interpretive perspective, researchers and practitioners have recently begun to highlight the intuitive, creative, practical and highly personalized nature of teachers' knowledge. In consequence, terms such as craft knowledge (McNamara and Desforges, 1978; Brown and McIntyre, 1992), practical knowledge (Elbaz, 1983), personal, practical knowledge (Connelly and Clandinin, 1988) and pedagogical content knowledge (Shulman, 1987) have all come to dominate the teaching agenda.

These conceptualizations stand in direct contrast to the earlier views of both Lortie (1975) and Jackson (1968), who argued that teachers lacked not only technical expertise but also anything approximating to professional knowledge. In this rather 'dismal' view of teachers' knowledge, the profession is shown to be 'insular, reliant on custom, whim, and immune to thoughtful reflection' (Liston and Zeichner, 1988, p. 62).

In order to explicate the complexities of these positions, this chapter is split into three sections, each with a particular focus: the first explores the role of knowledge in the classical professions, and looks at the extent to which such a model of knowledge production and knowledge use can be successfully applied to teaching; the second describes, in brief, the emergence of professional knowledge in teaching and the various epistemological claims that have been made on its behalf. This section ends with a survey of the current typifications that have been generated within the field of teacher knowledge. The third and final section considers how professional knowledge is used in the course of teaching, and the chapter closes with a summary of the main issues.

Knowledge and the professions

Numerous studies of the professions point to the centrality of a recognized body of knowledge as one of the formative criteria by which occupational groups can be categorized as professional. At the core of this classical conception is the notion that a profession bases its practice on a body of technical or specialist knowledge which is beyond the reach of lay people. Traditionally, this knowledge has two component parts: first, it has been tested by scientific method, thereby acquiring validity; second, it is supported by a variety of theoretical models and case descriptions which allow the knowledge to be applied to specific aspects in practice (Doyle, 1990a).

Put another way, professionals, through specialist and usually long periods of training, are taught to understand this research-validated knowledge and to apply it constructively and intelligently according to the ethical rules governing the conduct of the profession. In this sense, the established professions such as medicine and law, are able to label themselves professional and maintain their status and position in the occupational hierarchy.

Any discussion seeking to understand the relative merits and deployment of professional knowledge would do well to start with the medical profession. The analogy with medicine is a useful one because it articulates very clearly not only the problematic features of teaching, but also the problems of applying such a conception of professional knowledge to other occupational groups. In medicine, then, the practitioner is taught to take account of the universal laws of scientific procedure, particularly as they apply to chemistry, biology, physiology, etc. Thus, when attempting a diagnosis, doctors draw upon this putative body of knowledge to guide their actions. Although this model simplifies the process of diagnosis and downplays the role of experience and case knowledge, it is central to much of the professional training of medical practitioners (Pearson, 1989).

Although the primacy of this conception still holds in much of the medical establishment, further analysis has revealed that the principles and practice of medicine are not so integrated as the model suggests. Much of the problem arises from the distinction between the technical and practical elements of knowledge first outlined by Aristotle and further developed by Oakshott (1962). In this formulation, technical knowledge is seen as capable of some kind of written codification and resides in the learned journals and texts that surround the profession. Practical knowledge, on the other hand, is expressed in the act of practice and through reflection on those acts; this form of knowledge appears to defy codification, and is instead experiential and implicit (Eraut, 1988).

Building on these distinctions, Freidson, in his seminal study of the medical profession (1970), noted that in many respects the practitioner and the scientist inhabit different worlds; worlds that can be distinguished by a mentality born out of the distinct context within which they operate. Both, he claimed, had a fundamentally different view of the nature of knowledge and practice, and he hypothesized that the influence of the consulting room brought demands that meant that those

> whose work requires practical application to concrete cases cannot simply maintain the same frame of mind as the scholar or scientist: he cannot suspend action in the absence of incontrovertible evidence or be sceptical of himself, his experiences, his work and his fruit. In emergencies he cannot wait for the discoveries of the future. Dealing with individual cases, he cannot rely solely on probabilities or on general concepts or principles: he must also rely on his own senses. By the nature of his work the clinician must assume responsibility for practical action and in doing so he must rely on his concrete, clinical experience. (pp. 169–70)

Using this framework, Freidson went on to draw up typologies of both the clinician and the scientist, believing that, although textbook knowledge still maintains a hold over formal conceptions of diagnosis, of greater importance is the way in which the practitioner uses his case knowledge as a self-validating process to confirm or reject particular clinical actions. In this sense the burden of proof in cases is placed squarely on the shoulders of the practitioner, who has to take into account the particulars of the case rather than the general laws of the discipline.

In addition, other studies have pointed out further weaknesses in the scientific model, in that it ignores the many normative claims that are central to the practice of medicine. Values concerning prevention and appropriateness of technological health care, access to provision, and the myriad of ethical considerations surrounding the deployment and use of resources, all fail to appear in the classical underpinnings of medicine (Pearson, 1989).

47

In order to take into account these distinctions, Eraut (1988), in a reconceptualization of professional knowledge, focuses on the modes of knowledge use, harnessing Broudy *et al.*'s (1964) categories of acquired knowledge. The four modes – the replicative, the applicatory, the interpretive and the associative – all relate to the ways knowledge can be used in professional practice. The first represents the numerous routines that characterize professional life; the second is based on the ability of professionals to translate technical knowledge into prescriptions for action. The third is what might loosely be called wisdom and judgement (in other words, the ability of the professional to make efficacious decisions), while the fourth concentrates on the more indeterminate, intuitive modes of knowledge usually represented as the guiding metaphors and images that invoke particular meanings.

An analysis of the clinical context is also vital to our overall understanding of the issue of knowledge in the professions. Various typifications have been outlined, and these can be narrowed down to the academic, the policy-making and the action context (Eraut, 1988). All three have significance, but professional knowledge and professional practice are weakened when the boundaries between them are wide. Bernstein's (1971) collection code is a useful concept here; he claims that a greater integration of knowledge is likely to occur if the boundaries between the demarcations are weak rather than strong, thereby allowing a powerful collective code to emerge.

So, to what extent does teaching adhere to some of the principles of professional knowledge that characterize the medical profession? Are the various arms of the teaching profession related by a strong or a weak collective code?

The application of the medical model
When compared to the classical conception, teaching is usually considered to be inferior, and at best a semi-profession (Etzioni, 1969). However, the context-bound definition gives us more scope. In one sense, teaching does reflect many of the mores and complexities that characterize medicine; in particular, the

tendency towards indeterminacy, and the power and primacy of personal knowledge, judgement and responsibility. However, the analogy does become more difficult to sustain when we enter the debate about the generation of educational knowledge and its validity, and the uses to which that knowledge is put and its appropriacy. To understand this further we need to look in detail at the ways the two conceptions, the classical and the context-bound have been applied.

Those advocating the application of the classical conception of professional knowledge to education were likewise instrumental in trying to establish the universal laws of educational activity based on research and study in the four disciplines of human science, namely, psychology, sociology, philosophy and history. It was felt that the rooting of education in the social sciences would mirror the doctors' use of chemistry, physiology and biology as the base sciences for their knowledge production. It was maintained that research-validated knowledge would then become practice-orientated knowledge through a process of transformation by which information would be transferred from one arm of the profession to the other. Activating this rationalist view of professional knowledge, however, proved to be highly problematic.

For some, the lack of success was based on the fact that teachers consistently failed to utilize this core of specialized knowledge that had been developed on their behalf for over three decades. More recently, supporters of this view have admitted that in their enthusiasm they misunderstood many of the key variables that operate in classrooms, and that bridging the gap between knowledge and practice was more complex than they first realized. Nevertheless, one of the leading scholars in the area, Tom Good, has claimed in a recent book (1992), that research on teaching and learning has now reached such a sophisticated level that previous problems can be overcome and that the knowledge base can now guide teachers and help them solve their classroom problems.

For others, however, the indeterminacy of classrooms and the uncertainty of schools, combined with the diffuse and longitudinal nature of education (Carr and Kemmis, 1986), requires a wider range of skills, abilities, judgements and understandings that still cannot be narrowed down to a set of prescriptions for practice. The position is not made easier by the fact that many successful teachers, some of whom have never been formally trained, can often achieve success by apparently by-passing this 'stock of professional knowledge', relying instead on their own common sense, intuition and experience.

Furthermore, the emergence of a mass system of education pre-dated the formal study of education, and educationalists turned to academia to help them solve problems that had emerged within the structure rather than vice versa. In this sense, a large part of the practice of education developed without recourse to formal theory, whereas the practice of medicine grew up alongside scientific research, and advances in the field would have been impossible without scientific help. Thus medicine, unlike education, did not have to turn to science for help, it was already umbilically linked to it (O'Connor, 1973). Thus science set much of the medical agenda, while educational research often only provided clarification of already intractable problems. Also, a great deal of the research agenda in education was aimed at gaining academic respectability for education as a university subject, as well as being part of the teachers' drive for professional status (Pearson, 1989).

It appears, then, that despite the vast array of research findings on everything from 'time on task' to 'classroom with-it-ness', knowledge about teaching and learning adds up to only a fraction of the infinite number of variables, trade-offs and human nuances that make up the teacher–pupil relationship. And as Tom (1992), a well-known critic of such top-down approaches comments, 'Representing knowledge as a set of chunks of professional information does little to help the teacher make decisions within the intense framework of a classroom; neither does it help control the consequential indeterminacy of teacher–pupil relationships' (p. 24).

Such confusion among educationalists has, however, led numerous critics, particularly those on the right of the political spectrum, to call into question the value of educational knowledge and concomitant courses of professional training. For them, a grounding in the traditional professional knowledge of the teacher – the subject matter – combined with the support of a sympathetic and skilled teacher, together with plenty of on-the-job practice, is sufficient. The speed with which this barbaric idea has gained credence in some circles is impressive, and will be discussed at some length in the final chapter. However, of equal importance is the fact that much of the critique of educational knowledge has sprung from the profession's apparent inability to construct adequate warrants for the linking of theory and practice, an issue to which we will return.

The emergence of professional knowledge in teaching

The development of professional knowledge as a concept in education is inextricably linked to the rise of the schooled society (Wardle, 1974). During the late nineteenth and early twentieth century, schooling officially became professionalized as elementary and, to a lesser extent, secondary education came to dominate society's view of education. Schooling therefore became synonymous with social status, and individuals were defined by their levels of schooling (Doyle, 1990b).

An important element in this process was the eventual dominance of the education professional, who slowly but surely began to gain more control over the educational agenda as the century progressed. This perhaps reached its zenith in the notion of 'partnership', a concept that was to dominate teacher–state relations for three decades following the Second World War. Much of the validity of the educationists' claims concerning their control over the teaching and learning process was due in part to the emergence of educational theory, which was being increasingly linked to the rise of education as a university-based subject of study. The dissemination of much of this theory was carried out mainly through the traditional outlet of the academic and professional journal.

Initially, much of the literature was based on the ideas of the great theorists from Rousseau to Dewey, while later it found its natural home within the Psychology, Sociology, Philosophy and History of Education disciplines. In focusing on these four domains of knowledge, teaching could claim to be gathering intellectual respectability and professional status along the lines of the traditional professions. Applying the methodologies of the social-science disciplines therefore gave credence to much of the highly operationalized and fragmented theorizing that had preceded it.

Psychology in particular gained a special place, bringing as it did its theoretical frameworks about knowledge, learning and behaviour, many of which appeared central to the quest of teachers. It also introduced a methodological rigour, with its stress on measurement, extrapolation and analysis. Teaching and learning were therefore treated as generic processes, open to generalized conclusions and recommendations. Advocates thus believed that the results of psychological and sociological research could be transformed into a knowledge base which would serve teachers just as medical science served doctors.

During the 1970s much of the arm-linking was achieved through the rise of the 'curriculum package', where research findings and theory were reconstructed in the form of educational technology and resources. Such approaches were complemented by the rise of the Schools Council and other national projects. These were to be the conduits by which prevailing educational theory was transmitted and transformed into usable classroom activities. Although many of the projects were successful, professional knowledge as a unified concept still remained fragmented and peripheral.

By the late 1970s and 1980s there was a growing realization that the four disciplines' approach to professional knowledge, particularly as it was applied in initial teacher training, was increasingly irrelevant to the current and future needs of novice and experienced teachers. Nevertheless, much of the continued research activity remained wedded to the theoretical frameworks offered by the disciplines. The changes, however, also brought in their wake new conceptions of professional knowledge which challenged the top-down view inherent in the domains approach. Many of the emergent epistemologies directly opposed the dominant scientistic view of educational knowledge and chose instead to qualitatively explore and clarify the nature and significance of teachers' thinking and the knowledge that guides practice.

One major strand was the action-research movement, which placed the practitioner at the heart of the knowledge-production process. This group of scholars built their ideas on those advanced by Lewin (1946) and developed by Stenhouse (1975), and constructed a conception of knowledge that was context-specific and grew out of the systematic study, by practitioners, of their own practice. In this way, professional knowledge is articulated, understood and reflected upon within the process of teaching.

The results of much of this intense period of activity can be seen in the production of numerous taxonomies that purport to describe and delineate teachers' knowledge. Elbaz (1983) generated five categories of teachers' practical knowledge: knowledge of the self, knowledge of the milieu of teaching, knowledge of the subject matter, knowledge of the curriculum, and knowledge of instruction. Leinhardt and Smith (1985) categorized teacher knowledge using the propositional–procedural divide prevalent in cognitive psychology, and conceptualized teacher knowledge as being broken into subject-matter knowledge and knowledge of lesson structure. Shulman (1987) meanwhile defined seven categories of teacher knowledge: knowledge of the content, knowledge of pedagogy, knowledge of the curriculum, knowledge of learners and learning, knowledge of contexts of schooling, pedagogical content knowledge, and knowledge of educational philosophies, goals and objectives.

Regardless of the rival claims made by these various models, collectively they indicate not only a wide variety of epistemological underpinnings, but also reinforce the problematic nature of the whole concept of professional knowledge. Before going on to discuss some of the merits of these emergent models, and the relationships between them and the practice of teaching, we must briefly explore the three rival epistemologies that underpin their claims to validity.

Rival epistemologies

Positivist Although the construction of professional knowledge from a positivist perspective has come under attack in recent years, it still maintains its hold over much of the knowledge that is produced in education. In addition, the placing of professional knowledge within this paradigm has given it many advantages. First, it is felt that in creating value-free, law-like generalizations, the task of teaching and learning will be made more efficient. Second, it is believed that the application of the scientific method will create undisputed knowledge on a par with that of medicine; and third, this knowledge base will then complete the professional transformation of teaching and allow teachers to take their rightful place among the organized professions.

Thus the generation of context-free generalizations is sought, and the laws inferred from such generalizations are intended to provide the answers to the practitioners' problems. However, the separation of practice from research, and the importance of context in the process of teaching, has meant that such approaches have had a limited effect. Nevertheless, the tradition remains strong, despite its apparently uneasy fit with the world of the practitioner.

Interpretive Much of the epistemological basis of the interpretive paradigm is rooted in the phenomenological philosophy of Husserl and Schutz. This perspective challenged the foundational ontological assumptions of positivism; a process which led to a radical reappraisal of the nature of knowledge, knowledge creation and knowledge use in the human sciences. Branching out from this phenomenological root are a variety of related epistemological offshoots, including the existentialism of Sartre, Heidegger and Merleau-Ponty, the interactionism of

George Herbert Mead, the ethnomethodology of Garfinkel, the hermeneutics of Gadamer and Ditthey, and the phenomenography of Martons.

Despite the problem of conceptual and methodological distinctions, common to all the perspectives is the urge to understand the social world and those who inhabit it in terms of their inter-subjective levels of consciousness. Thus the paradigm seeks to understand, describe and explain the inner realms of human consciousness, motivation and intentionality using a variety of methodological tools.

At the core of this ideographic approach is the detailed case study, comprising participant observations, structured and unstructured interviews. Unlike positivists, who try to cleanse their studies of corrupting influences, the interpretive researcher places values and attitudes at the heart of the research enterprise and, seeks to describe and explain phenomena in the light of those underlying variables.

Critical Dissatisfaction with the positivist and interpretive traditions led numerous scholars and researchers to formulate an alternative, more wide-ranging paradigm as the basis for the development of professional knowledge. Based essentially on the work of Habermas, this orientation placed values at the heart of its thoughts and actions. Scholarship within this tradition calls for a radical rethink of the numerous assumptions that underpin educational policy-making and practice. Drawing on Habermas's construct of 'knowledge constitutive interests', scholars have sought to define knowledge as being socially, economically and politically constructed, and therefore tied to fundamental structural interests.

This knowledge is constructed along three levels which make up Habermas's conception: the technical, the personal, and the emancipatory. The first represents the intrinsic interest of individuals who feel the need to gather knowledge that will help them control their world; the second level is seen as allowing individuals to act and perform judgements about their immediate environment; the third requires higher-order thinking which overcomes the solipsism of the phenomeno-logists and relates an emancipatory knowledge within which social and political change can occur. According to Carr and Kemmis (1986), it is with this final, transformative category that critical theory is essentially concerned.

Although these rival epistemologies are often counterposed, much of the research and thinking done in relation to teachers' professional knowledge rarely draws on one tradition exclu-sively. Admittedly, the process-product paradigm was rooted firmly in positivist notions of knowledge, more particularly behaviourist psychology, but many of the others have adopted a more eclectic position. McCutcheon (1981) has claimed that instead of the three traditions being seen as polar, they should be viewed as part of an eternal triangle along the dimensions of which a variety of researchers and scholars operate. This eclecticism is visible when an analysis is made of the more recent typifications of professional knowledge.

Typifications of professional knowledge

Before outlining in detail these explicatory frameworks and their underlying assumptions, it is important to point out that the studies referred to in this section are only a small representa-tion of the wide variety of literature available. To aid understanding, this section has been split into five subsections, each representing the particular focus of the studies. These are: the cognitive, the practical, the biographical, the contextual, and the subject.

The cognitive

Research on teachers' professional knowledge is a recent pheno-menon, and emerged out of the process-product tradition begun in the 1960s. The shortcomings of that paradigm signalled a shift in emphasis from the preoccupation with what teachers *do* to an attempt to uncover what they know about teaching and learning, and the ways in which such knowledge is acquired, developed and used. This change in orientation brought in its wake a similar shift in methodology; a process initially dominated by the growing concern to understand both cognition and context (Carter, 1990).

The influence of the former grew into what became known as the teachers' thinking paradigm, which sought to investigate the complexity of cognitive processes used by teachers in their daily work. Relying on concepts drawn from information-processing studies and cognitive psychology, investigators used flexible data collection methods, including task-setting and analysis, process traces and stimulated recall.

Early studies concentrated on what Clark and Yinger (1988) have called 'the hidden world of teaching', or what Jackson (1968) labelled the 'pre-active phase' of teaching. These investigations tried to explicate the thinking behind the complex decisions teachers make routinely in their pre-teaching preparation. Results showed that teachers engage in two main activities: the first is associated with the types of planning used, and ranges from yearly to termly to monthly, to weekly, to daily and to individual lessons. Within these types teachers took account of important factors including activities, content, pupils' abilities as well as short-and long-term learning objectives. The second highlighted the complex cognitive processes involved in planning, and found that during this phase teachers solved potential classroom problems, orientated their activities towards learning, and made decisions about both content and process. In so doing, teachers it seems, draw on their prior experiences to help them create lessons, a process often carried out with the help of images of particular teaching episodes which are called up according to the demands of the present.

Findings from these studies appeared to contradict many previously held assumptions about planning and teaching. For decades the Tylerian or rational planning model had been the mainstay of many courses of professional training. However, research seemed to show that teachers' planning rarely moved in a linear pattern; instead it meandered, allowing past problems, previous ideas and possible solutions to interweave in a complex dialogue with present predicaments. The choices made were affected by the routines that had been inculcated, together with the perceived needs of the class and the demands of the curriculum. Thus teachers, it seems, rarely begin with objectives, preferring instead to start with perhaps content or with the activities which would engage the class.

In terms of interactive thinking, studies using stimulated recall and observation methods have attempted to understand the basis of teachers' decision-making in the classroom. Investigations have varied in their complexity: some have focused on the number of decisions made about classroom constants, whereas others have homed in on the contextual variables that influenced teachers' thinking. Findings suggest that teachers try to inculcate particular routines early on in the academic year and build their thinking up deliberately, thus cutting down on the need for improvisation and complex decision-making during interactive teaching.

In the expert–novice tradition, results have shown experienced teachers' knowledge to be based firmly on a series of typifications which define classroom events. In this sense, pupils' behaviour, modes of learning and classroom management are all understood with reference to a highly elaborate system of stimuli, and in consequence improvised behaviour is controlled and used within a highly structured system of routines. This event-structured knowledge is experiential, rich in images and patterns, and is highly specialized and domain-specific, as well as being organized and stored in the form of scenes and procedures (Carter 1990).

The practical
Much of the thrust of the information-processing approach to teachers' knowledge was systematically to clarify the complexity of a great deal of the tacit professional knowledge of teachers. In contrast to the cognitive and deliberative approach used in many of the studies, research on teachers' personal practical knowledge and implicit theories has tended to draw on phenomenology for its concepts and methodology.

Using the social phenomenology of Shutz, Elbaz (1983) published a detailed case study of one teacher's practical knowledge. Using interviews and observations, she characterized practical knowledge as being made up of five broad domains: the self, the milieu of teaching, the subject matter, the curriculum, and finally instruction. Cutting across these categories, she identified three levels of generality which help organize this knowledge: the first consists of rules of practice, the second is made up of practical principles, and the third consists of images which when combined make up 'the teacher's feelings, values, needs and beliefs' (p. 134). Of central importance in the study was the fact that Elbaz was less concerned with what the teacher knew in terms of propositional or procedural knowledge, but was more concerned with the characteristics of her professional knowledge and the connections between the self and the conditions of teaching.

Building on the work of Elbaz, Connelly and Clandinin (1988) introduced the extended construct of personal practical knowledge to describe the personal understandings teachers have of their practical contexts. In order to bring this knowledge into the public domain, Connelly and Clandinin explored, usually collaboratively, specific teaching episodes and the ways in which the personal practical knowledge of teachers interacts with events, thereby producing professional knowledge. Of central importance is the concept of image, which is further defined as something which 'draws both the past and the future, into a personally meaningful nexus of experience focused on the immediate situation that called it forth' (1985, p. 198).

This form of knowledge is inextricably bound up with the knower and is inseparable from his or her experiences, both personal and professional. The researchers thus use narrative enquiry to explore the personal realms of teachers' knowledge, a process which focuses on the experiential details of practice and includes recollections of previous positions and generic life experiences as well as the theoretical representations required to account for it. This 'shift' in focus from the outside to the inside is an attempt to create a more unified, holistic, coherent and integrated conception of professional knowledge; in short, a truly authentic view of practice that will not only promote change in the individual but will also serve as a model for further study and personal explorations.

The biographical

This category, although closely associated with the practical tradition outlined above, has significant methodological and epistemological differences. The majority of biographical or life-history studies try to uncover and clarify the development and deployment of teachers' knowledge in relation to the socio-political and economic backdrop of their work. Much of the life-history work has followed Denizen's (1991) remark that 'life history may be the best method for studying adult socialization, the situational response of the self to daily interactional contingencies' (p. 7). The orientation also grew up in response to many of the persistent problems surrounding the relationship between teachers' working lives and the educational theory being offered to them as solutions to those issues. Peter Woods (1987), a prominent researcher in the field, summarized the problems thus:

1. Much of the research-based knowledge produced on behalf of teachers was in reality very remote from their practical concerns.

2. The deficit view of professional knowledge often depicted teachers as weak professionals, unable to act rationally according to the set rules.

3. Much of the knowledge was formulaic and ignored the highly personalized and biographical nature of teachers' knowledge.

4. The experiences of teachers and the interactions of the personal-professional elements of their lives were given little significance in the conceptualizations of teaching that had already emerged in the research literature.

Life-history approaches to educational research formed part of the backlash against the ascendancy of positivist epistemologies of the 1960s and 1970s, and grew up alongside the phenomenological, interactionist and ethnographic traditions that were becoming increasingly popular in research circles. Life history, as Goodson (1992) points out, offers historical depth to ethnography and allows wider political, social and economic circumstances to be explored within the personal lives and experiences of individual teachers. Of central importance to this conception of professional knowledge is the notion of the self and the ways in which the self gains currency within a career focus; in the long term, the facilitation of this personal understanding then becomes the engine for further professional development and curricular change.

A variety of approaches have been utilized to explore what Pinar (1988) has called the 'architecture of the self'. Individual and collaborative autobiography (Pinar, 1988) and biography (Butt and Raymond, 1987) have been popular. Here researchers and teachers work together to create and interpret their life experiences, thereby developing a basis for an understanding of practice within its wider context. A major concern is to clarify and celebrate the practitioner's voice so that policy changes and pedagogical initiatives are made with reference to the teacher's experience.

Others locate their studies within the wider career histories of teachers. Such accounts draw on ethnographic and interactionist principles to understand the power and prominence of latent culture and how such forces influence practice. Thus, by exploring the 'critical incidents' and the substantive and situated identities of teachers, researchers such as Ball and Goodson (1985) claim to be catapulting the teacher to the forefront of the educational exercise.

The contextual

An alternative angle has seen professional knowledge conceptualized as contextual; in other words, the ways in which the variables of the classroom interact with the teacher's understandings to produce 'ecological knowledge'. Studies in this field have investigated the concept of academic work and the knowledge and understandings teachers use to create order and a learning environment within their classrooms. From this perspective, professional knowledge is a two-way process, and one in which events, as well as the teacher's understanding of those events, interact to produce learning. Walter Doyle, a leading figure in this movement, has focused his endeavours on what he terms (1983) 'the tasks of teaching', factors which he identifies as foundational elements in the way teachers sustain order and in the way they steer pupils through the curriculum.

In an earlier clarification of contextual knowledge, Doyle (1977) shows teachers' professional knowledge to be event-structured, in other words, teachers' knowledge of content, teaching techniques and classroom management strategies is linked to specific events they have already experienced in their classrooms. Teachers, it is claimed, organize their thinking during planning and teaching around specific chunks of content, and create curriculum scripts. According to Doyle (1990a), this knowledge is 'particularistic and situational', is founded on case histories and based on two interrelated images: the first sees teaching as a process of reproducing and enacting the curriculum in the classroom; the second captures teaching as a problem-solving enterprise based on the utilization of case knowledge.

Yinger (1987) has also tried to capture this knowledge, and using the term 'improvisation' he argues that experienced teachers have the capacity to think on their feet and make sense of problematic situations by bringing their vast repertoire of past experiences and similar cases to the forefront of their minds during interactive teaching. This improvised knowledge, he claims, is difficult to codify and articulate in any ordered way, and research into it needs a more sophisticated methodology in order to develop a language of practice that can be communicated.

In a similar vein, Brown and McIntyre (1992) set out to explore the 'ordinary things which experienced teachers do spontaneously in their classrooms', the long-term aim being to exemplify 'that part of teachers' professional knowledge which is acquired primarily through their practical experience, is brought to bear spontaneously and, routinely on their teaching, and so guides their day to day actions in the classroom'. This they refer to as 'teachers' professional craft knowledge' (p. 39). Their study of sixteen experienced teachers from a variety of disciplines found that teachers often judged their actions in terms of their ability to create a stable environment in which pupil activity could flourish. This they defined as a 'Normally Desirable State' (NDS). Second, the teachers in the study had a wide repertoire of approaches and strategies which they drew upon to attain their short-term aims. The choice of these actions depended on the level of NDS they wished to achieve, as well as being connected to their own interpretation of the situations in which they found themselves. The link between these goals and actions was not, however, axiomatic, for 'rarely did teachers have a single goal in mind and single tactics for attaining them' (p. 112).

The subject

Traditionally, the professional knowledge of teachers has rested to a certain extent on their knowledge of their subject. For decades the dictum 'knowing one's subject' was deemed to be sufficient for most teachers to be allowed to practice; indeed, in many of our top public schools this is still the case. Although in recent years teaching has been characterized as a complex process, many persist in believing that a good knowledge of the subject combined with on-the-job practice is sufficient for success in the classroom (O'Hear, 1988; Lawlor, 1990).

Historically, this simplified conception was seen to be based on the interaction of three variables: the teacher, the subject and the pupil. However, more than thirty years of educational research and reform have altered this cosy image of the teaching-learning process. New concepts of teaching, combined with the findings of research on learning, saw teaching transformed from a process based on knowledge transmission to one based on knowledge construction. Increasingly, the teacher as deliverer was replaced with notions of the teacher as facilitator or task manager; in these new definitions subject knowledge was viewed as only one of a number of competing elements which made up teachers' professional knowledge.

The effects of these changes were perhaps best exhibited in the primary sector. There the curriculum came to be organized around themes or areas of experience, and subjects were converged to create clusters or blocks of study. This was justified by the argument that a subject-centred view of the curriculum contrasted sharply with the child's view of the world, which, it was deemed, was both holisitic and integrated. The kind of teacher that emerged from this conception was someone who was a facilitator of children's learning, and one who should teach the whole curriculum. In contrast, at secondary level subject knowledge and understanding remained central, despite attempts to extend the integrated concepts, so prevalent in the primary school, across the binary divide.

Of late, there has been a resurgence of interest in the subject knowledge of teachers. On both sides of the Atlantic new curricula have seen traditional subject culture being placed at the heart of the curriculum. This has meant that the 'missing paradigm' (Shulman, 1987) on research on teachers' professional knowledge – the subject – has come back into focus. In Britain, David McNamara (1990) has claimed that too often there has been a tendency to see 'teaching and learning as generic activities without reference to the subject knowledge which provides the substantive content for learners' (p. 113). Similarly, Bennett and Carre (1991), reporting on an investigation into student teachers' subject-matter knowledge, claimed that 'teachers need such knowledge to adequately transform programmes of study and attainment targets into worthwhile and appropriate tasks, they need it to frame accurate and high quality explanations and they need it to diagnose accurately children's understandings and misconceptions'.

Investigations into teachers' subject knowledge and understandings have also made the important conceptual distinction between subject-matter knowledge *per se* and subject-matter knowledge for teaching. Wilson *et al.* (1987) have shown that such knowledge is not simply propositional and factual, but includes the conceptual underpinning of the subject and the belief structures that each teacher holds in relation to it. Ball (1990) refers to this distinction as knowledge of the subject and knowledge about the subject. The latter includes knowledge about the ways of best representing the content so that it fosters learning. Thus subject-matter knowledge for teaching includes knowledge of what pupils bring to the classroom and knowledge of the ways pupils solve particular problems in each subject area. It also includes ideas about pupils' prior conceptions and the common misconceptions that affect their learning.

It is this complex amalgam that Shulman (1987) has called 'pedagogical content knowledge'; a concept he defines as the teacher's ability to make the content penetrable for pupils. Shulman's discussion suggests that expertise in teaching requires knowledge not only of the substantive and syntactic knowledge of the subject, but also an integrated and conceptual understanding of the domain itself. Thus pedagogical content knowledge is unique to teachers and forms a central part of their professional knowledge.

Professional knowledge and teaching

We will now consider some of the problems that are inherent in the relationship between professional knowledge and the act of teaching, often called the theory–practice divide. In this section we explore three different theoretical positions. We begin with a brief excursion to the normative theory of Paul Hirst, this is followed by a discussion of Gary Fenstermacher's practical arguments position, and the section ends with a brief explanation of Donald Schon's concept of reflective practice.

For Paul Hirst (1984), theory is a 'set or system of rules or a collection of precepts which guide or control actions of various kinds' (p. 2). In this sense educational theory can be seen as a broad church of ideas and principles which includes both the academic-scientific as well as the practical and experiential. This inclusive definition also places equal value on practice, and, as Hirst (1990) points out, problems usually begin in practical situations and in the rules and principles that practitioners employ in their judgements and justifications for action. Recast this way, educational theory becomes a body of professional knowledge that deals with the actions of teachers, while at the same time helping them to understand what they do. He comments:

> What matters then in assessing human action or the activities or practices they comprise is not whether or not they are informed by theory in this general sense, but whether that theory is any good. . . . From these elementary considerations it is then a simple step to recognising that the professional activities that any teacher engages in are what they are by virtue of the theory that informs them, by virtue of the concepts, beliefs and principles that the teacher employs. And whether that teacher is indeed acting professionally turns on whether that theory is rationally defensible in terms of the best knowledge and understanding of such situations and of what ought to be done in such circumstances. (1990, p. 75)

Hirst offers two criteria for judging such activities as 'rationally defensible': first, practical principles must be able to stand up to a practical test; second, these practical principles must be justified in terms of current knowledge and values.

Hirst further claims that professional practice needs to be developed in such a way that 'parallels the development of technological practices, their structuring by means of informally conceived theory giving place to structuring in systematically developed practical theory that is defensible by reference to experiments in practice informed by the basic disciplines' (p. 83). He therefore concludes that if teaching is ever to become truly professional, then there is a pressing need to develop a necessary body of practices informed by and 'justified by a defensible domain of practical theory' (p. 83). While recognizing the contingent nature of teaching, Hirst claims that as part of their professional code teachers should possess a rationally understood position in relation to practice which would not only act as a bulwark against state interference, but also be a major weapon in their professional armoury. In this sense a justification for practice is made in relation to the best knowledge available, and in relation to the moral, ethical, socioeconomic and political contexts within which teachers operate. It is here, claims Hirst, that formal educational theory as generated through the disciplines can provide a basis for understanding.

Gary Fenstermacher (1986) offers a similar view of the relationship between theory and practice. Central to his conceptualization, however, is the distinction between the generation and the application of knowledge. For him, the former consists of statements of propositions about the world which are made tenable by the mediating effect of the methodology of a particular paradigm; the latter meanwhile consists of statements tied to actions. Fenstermacher goes on to outline two examples by which the distinction is made more explicit. The first 'knowledge production argument' goes something like this: 'research has indicated that learning is likely to occur in well managed classrooms. There is evidence that direct instruction is effective for classroom management. Therefore learning is more likely to occur in classrooms that incorporate direct method' (p. 42). The 'knowledge use argument', on the other hand, moves in a slightly different direction:

> as a teacher, I want to teach in ways that yield as much
> student learning as possible. Well managed classrooms yield
> gains in learning. Direct instruction is a proven way to manage
> a classroom. My students and I are together in this classroom.
> **Action:** I will organize my class according to the principles of
> direct methods.   (p. 42)

The differences between the two are, according to Fenstermacher, that the first consists of a set of assertions, while the second, although also having assertions, some of which are empirically testable, is in the end pointed in the direction of action. This form of practical reasoning he calls 'the philosophy of pragmatism'.

Furthermore, Fenstermacher maintains that the distinction

between the two gives the educational researcher the freedom to explore questions of a purely academic nature as long as he or she meets the criteria of adequacy imposed on the discipline by its methodology. Such research, he emphasizes, should not be bound by a concern for the practical or pedagogical effects of the enquiry, and he asserts that his position is based on the proposition that improvements in practice will only be realized if there are corresponding improvements in the practical arguments put forward for those actions. Such a claim appears to argue against the direct application of findings from research to practice and instead puts the emphasis on the development of practical reasoning by the teacher. In this way research-validated knowledge is useful in that it can change 'the truth value of the premises of the practical argument in the mind of the teacher' (p. 43). Research then influences practice because it alters the truth or falsity of beliefs that teachers may have, and further holds out the possibility of changing the nature of those beliefs as well as adding new ones.

To illustrate his thesis, Fenstermacher offers an example of a teacher who, while being committed to resource-based, individualized, child-centred learning, realizes that despite her beliefs her pupils are not performing well in the end of term tests. So despite setting up her classroom to reflect her beliefs and values, she is faced with a dilemma: should she experiment and change her classroom organization so that the pupils might score higher in the tests, or maintain her beliefs despite doubts? The teacher begins to read process-product research literature and finds that the results show individualized learning not to be congruent with high test marks. The research is therefore being used to modify the practical premises of the teacher's practical arguments; but the decision to change will not rely on that information alone, for, as Fenstermacher claims, practices will not change simply by applying lessons from the findings of research, and the best that can be hoped for is modification.

Instead, the teacher's practical arguments and reasoning, which encompass intuitive, reflective, ethical and moral perspectives of action, are only the methods for transforming what is empirically known into practice. Thus the main criteria applied to show the benefit of theory should be the improvements made in the practical arguments of teachers.

One solution dismissed by Fenstermacher for solving this problem is that the gap between researchers and practitioners be closed and that greater collaboration should emerge between the two arms of the profession. This he claims is a 'profound misconception'. For him the work of the researcher will not be improved by imposing constraints from the world of practice, nor will practitioners be advantaged by conceiving of their task in terms of research. Thus each is held accountable only for what it is possible for each to do, for 'the yield of professional knowledge can never fully be subordinated to the needs of practice' (p. 44).

Putting this argument into practice, Fenstermacher adopts the analogy of the teaching and learning process in the classroom. Here he feels that helping teachers develop practical arguments requires researchers and academics to engage with the teachers and help them develop reasoned belief, understanding, autonomy and authenticity in terms of their pedagogical competence. One of the first actions should be to help teachers frame the often implicit practical arguments underpinning their practice; next, teacher educators should help teachers appraise the premisses upon which their practical arguments are based: a process that may very well include the introduction of empirical evidence. The teacher educator therefore bases his or her actions on morally defensible and rationally justifiable courses of action, a process that militates against the willy-nilly introduction of research-based knowledge. He concludes that

The role of educational research, when it is done well, is to help us know and understand a certain limited range of educational phenomena. This knowledge and understanding from research may improve educational practice if it bears fruitfully on the premisses of practical arguments in the minds of teachers. (p. 47)

In contrast, Donald Schon, in two highly influential books,

The Reflective Practitioner (1983) and *Educating the Reflective Practitioner* (1987), constructed a critique of existing professional knowledge based on an alternative epistemology of practice. His analysis begins with an attack on the basis of traditional, rational forms of professional knowledge, a process he terms technical rationality:

> According to the model of technical rationality – the view of professional knowledge which has most powerfully shaped both our thinking about the professions and the institutional relations of research, education and practice – professional activity consists in instrumental problem solving made rigorous by the application of scientific theory and technique.   (1983, p. 21)

In opposition, Schon depicts practice as ambiguous, value laden and open to multifarious interpretations and actions. In this messy world of practice, the end–means model of professional knowledge is at best irrelevant and at worst dangerous. The emergence and acceptance of this technical view of professional knowledge is, according to Schon, based on the positivist notion of the power of predictability to control human affairs. However, he is cautious in his attack on science and maintains that one should draw a careful distinction between science *per se* and the positivist view of science. For Schon, it is the latter which dominates, because, he claims, we tend to see science after the fact, as a body of

> established propositions derived from research. When we recognise their limited utility in practice, we experience the dilemma of rigour and relevance. But we may also consider science before the fact as a process in which scientists grapple with uncertainties and display arts of inquiry akin to the uncertainties and arts of practice.   (1983, p. 44)

Schon is essentially interested in the basis of skilful practice and the process of professional problem-solving in the world of commonplace situations which are endemically unstable, unique and value laden. He is thus attempting to construct an epistemology that honours the intuitive, implicit processes that are at the heart of intelligent practice. At the core of his conception is the notion of tacit understanding, and building on the work of Polanyi he outlines the basis of intuitive performance and the importance of the knowledge implicit in everyday actions:

> When we go about the spontaneous, intuitive performance of
> the actions of everyday life, we show ourselves to be
> knowledgeable in a special way. Often we cannot say what it is
> that we know. When we try to describe it, we find ourselves
> at a loss, or we produce descriptions that are obviously
> inappropriate. Our knowing is ordinarily tacit, implicit in our
> patterns of action and in our feel for the stuff with which we
> are dealing. It seems right to say that our knowing is in our
> action.   (1983, p. 49)

Seen in this way, the art of practice is situated within the confines of performance, and Schon both honours and celebrates the *in situ* competence and artistry of the professional. Furthermore, claims Schon, the practitioner is often unaware of this tacit knowledge, and, having learned the skill intuitively, describing it becomes problematic and complex. In order to make use of that knowledge, Schon introduces the concept of 'reflection-in-action' as a means by which professional knowledge is brought into the fray of professional decision-making; this is represented as a process of problem-setting and problem-solving. Thus in the real world of practice, problems do not simply present themselves coldly to the practitioner, they have to be constructed from the artefacts or problematic situations which are 'puzzling, troubling and uncertain' (1983, p. 40). He goes on to say:

> When we set the problem, we select what we will treat as the
> things of the situation, we set the boundaries of our attention
> to it, and we impose upon it a coherence which allows us to
> say what is wrong and in what directions the situation needs to
> be changed. Problem setting is a process in which interactively
> we name the things to which we will attend and frame the
> context in which we will attend to them.   (p. 40)

71

The methodological underpinning to reflection-in-action is the reflective conversation, whereby the practitioner brings past experiences to bear on present problems. Here frames are imposed which highlight the problematic nature of practice, so just as the problem is being set solutions begin to present themselves. Central to this process is the art of experimentation, which is an attempt by the practitioner to 'see what can be made to follow from a re-framing of a situation' so as to 'adapt the situation to the frame'. In this way reflection-in-action involves a dialectic interchange between the practitioner and the situation, a process by which the practitioner's moves produce 'unintended changes which give the situation new meaning'. Here the 'situation talks back, the practitioner listens, and as he approaches what he hears, he re-frames the situation once again' (p. 145).

This definition of experimentation contrasts with the hypothetico-deductive approach found in the natural sciences. Schon takes issue with that approach to the human sciences and provides from a variety of professional contexts a number of case accounts of reflective experimentation and the logic behind it. And in so doing he broadly outlines three types of experimentation.

1. *The exploratory experiment.* This is seen as broadly equating to the basic experimentation associated with direct immediate results. For instance, a teacher alters the classroom seating arrangements from rows to groups to see if it has positive or negative effects on classroom mood.

2. *The move-testing experiment.* Here the changes to the practical situation are done in order to see if particular changes will result from the experiment. The teacher, for instance, rearranges the gender balance of groups to see if improved interaction takes place.

3. *Hypothesis testing.* Although the basis for such experimentation is similar to that employed in technical rationality, the very fact that such an experiment takes place within the confines of practice and that the teacher is part of the experiment and does not deny his or her involvement marks it out as

different. For example, a teacher hypothesizes that allowing children greater choice over their work will bring about greater quality of performance and sets up an experiment to test the validity of that claim. Despite the teacher being part of the research process and wanting it to succeed, the situation, according to Schon, acts as a counter-weight against the dangers of self-fulfilment.

Schon's work has rapidly become highly influential and has led to a considerable rethink of the role of professional knowledge in teaching. The notion of intelligent performance and the stress placed on professional judgement appears to offer teachers the chance to recapture the professional agenda while at the same time giving them the opportunity to celebrate and make explicit a great deal of the knowledge and expertise that resides within their practice.

Conclusions

As we have shown, the relationship between formal research-validated knowledge constructed by academics and the action-related world of the practitioner is still central to much of the debate about the nature of professional knowledge. The problem is in part related to the impossibility of providing a set of answers to the infinite number of problems and tensions that are thrown up daily in every classroom. Nevertheless, we believe there is now a sufficient sophistication within the various methodologies to produce what amounts to a considerable body of professional knowledge that can help practitioners think about and remedy many of the classroom problems they face. Integrating this knowledge with the uniqueness of their own personal and contextual understandings is an important challenge for all those involved in the initial and further professional development of teachers. However, if this solution seems less than rigorous, as Edwards (1992) points out, it is because pedagogy is a less than precise art, and such imprecision is part of the 'unavoidable consequence of the

73

messiness and unpredictability of the problems to which it relates' (p. 288).

In addition, the continued professionalization of teaching also depends to a large extent on the 'public acceptance of the legitimacy of what the occupation asserts about itself' (Doyle, 1990b, p. 8). This factor is dependent on two interlocking processes: first, teachers must be seen to have some kind of social and educational impact; second, they must demonstrate that they have the technical, reflective and ethical qualities necessary to handle their task. If teachers are to maintain and develop their professionality in line with these two factors, public confidence can be gained only if the profession openly asserts its expertise, a process which can be given greater credibility by the existence of a recognized body of professional knowledge.

Of late, teachers have been subjected to considerable state pressure to conform to an accountability structure which has done much to undermine their traditional workplace autonomy. Being put on the defensive has forced a major rethink of their position, and here the stock of professional knowledge which has emerged over the past two decades may carry vital symbolic as well as practical significance by helping them to re-establish their public esteem.

The medical profession has come under similar pressures, though not of the same magnitude, and the possession of such a corpus has insulated its members from attacks on their status and has provided them with a barrier against an overbearing state. An important element here is the correspondence between doctors' professional knowledge and their occupational status. In this sense teachers' professional knowledge has always been plagued by a credibility gap. As Tedd Wragg continually reminds us, the great unknowing public would not dream of carrying out a surgical operation after a few days observing in an operating theatre. Likewise, they would never consider flying a jumbo jet after a few hours in the flight simulator. Yet the same unknowing public probably believes that given a bit of practice they could teach a class of children reasonably effectively. These powerful latent beliefs, coming as they do from a long 'apprenticeship of observation' (Lortie, 1975) as a pupil, have done much to undermine and influence public perception of the expertise needed to be a successful teacher.

Furthermore, in medicine, the possession of an accepted stock of secret knowledge, regardless of its utility or veracity, has become ingrained in a network of common cultural expectations. Such a corpus not only works in the best interests of that particular occupational group by ensuring its status, but it also guides its relationship to and control of the educational institutions that provide the knowledge, and the occupational, social and political frameworks that reward it.

For this reason alone, teachers need to have such a body of knowledge, not only for its power to help them construct practical arguments and rationally defensible positions, but also because it is part of what the public and they themselves see as part of being professional. Denying them that right, whether it be from the side of the controlling state or from the moralizing of academics, will in the long term be counter-productive.

In all professions the crucial link between the practitioner and the client is based on mutual trust and belief in the power of the practitioner's judgement to use his or her specialist knowledge efficaciously. Teachers, as we have pointed out, work overwhelmingly in organizations and have a fragmented and complex relationship with their clientele. Having to work simultaneously with large numbers in a longitudinal sense makes for a different set of relationships than those that arise in the traditional professional consulting-room context. For teachers, the power of the organization – the school – to dictate much of that relationship is vital, and they can never come close to acting in the highly individualistic ways that characterize other professions. Thus, whereas doctors and lawyers make their own decisions and apply their stock of professional knowledge often in controlled conditions, teachers have daily to negotiate their way through a minefield of human, institutional and social relationships.

By grounding professional knowledge within the 'wisdom of practice' (Elliot, 1990), it is hoped that teachers will be able to overcome the problems posed by these fluid relationships and gain some semblance of control over their professional destiny. The popularity of such a conception, particularly among teacher educators and some educational academics, is based on an emancipatory perspective which it is believed will lead to greater personal-professional empowerment.

Critics, on the other hand, see such developments as raising tensions which go to the very heart of professionalism. First, if professional practice is to be accountable, and it has to be, then professional knowledge must be more than the sum of its parts; in effect, the proclamation of reflective practice may be leading teachers down a blind alley where teaching and reflecting simply become routine matters and where practice itself is never tested against a broader public context of ideas and issues. In this sense, reflective practice is construed as narrow and personal, lacking in public defensibility and offering no safe indicator of expertise. Thus a teacher may be very reflective but also ineffective in the classroom; and although reflection is a necessary element in teachers' professional knowledge, it is by no means sufficient (Day, 1993). So encouraging teachers to be reflective practitioners (whatever that may mean) may be limiting them to the confines of their personal knowledge and to a private engagement with it.

Perhaps the problem lies in the tendency of those involved in debates about professional knowledge (usually academics) to demonstrate a strong preference for constructing that knowledge according to one or more of the particular epistemologies. This chapter has shown that such positions have numerous implications, and that taking too narrow a view could jeopardize any future attempts at regaining some semblance of control over the educational agenda.

4 The issue of autonomy

Practitioner autonomy is central to the idea of a profession. The argument has been set out previously in Chapter 1 but can be briefly restated as follows: as professionals work in uncertain situations in which judgement is more important than routine, it is essential to effective practice that they should be sufficiently free from bureaucratic and political constraints to act on judgements made in the best interests (as they see them) of the clients. The arguments against autonomy have also been briefly referred to in Chapter 1. These can be summarized as follows: professional practice is more predictable and subject to evaluation than professional interest groups allow, and their claims for autonomy are, in fact, strategies for the avoidance of accountability and the involvement of clients in dialogue about practice.

The above summary presents autonomy versus accountability as a zero-sum issue. It is not, of course. In reality one is concerned with *degrees* of autonomy and hence with *degrees* of uncertainty in professional practice. Solutions will take the form of the nicely calculated less or more, rather than of stringent limits on autonomy or unbridled freedom for the practitioner. Nevertheless, calculations have to be made since educational policy, legislation and management strategies must attempt to resolve the issue. The present chapter will consider this balance by exploring the degree of unpredictability which is inherent in professional practice in education, and the nature and extent of teacher autonomy which follows from this analysis.

The concept of professional autonomy

In this chapter we consider professional autonomy to be the relative freedom enjoyed by practitioners in making and implementing choices regarding their professional practice. Some further comments on this usage are in order.

Professional autonomy is a limited form of autonomy. Although it can be seen as embedded in a wider range of ethical and political issues, these will not be pursued here (see Lindley, 1986; Dworkin, 1988, for wider discussions of autonomy; and White, 1990, for autonomy as an aim of education).

Professional autonomy is always constrained. Practitioners do not have licence, but have *a* licence. This licence to practise is based upon demonstrated competence and is conditional. Limitations are also inherent in professional ethics, as are the rights of clients.

Professional autonomy is variable over place and time. In England and Wales perhaps the apotheosis of teacher autonomy was attained in the 1960s, with constraints on professional practice increasing from the emergence of the accountability movement in the mid-1970s.

The form of professional autonomy is contextual. In the case of teaching, the principal contexts are the classroom and the school, which, of course, overlap. In the classroom, the areas in which a teacher can have a greater or lesser degree of autonomy include the following: aims, topics, materials, teaching styles and strategies, allocation of time within and between lessons, modes of assessment, standards of achievement, etc., etc. Some of these areas will be matters of school policy rather than individual choice, and hence the autonomy of the school (i.e. the collectivity of head and teachers) becomes an issue, as does the nature and degree of participation of teachers in decision-making about school policy – which may entail a loss of individual autonomy in the interests of greater collective autonomy.

Professional autonomy is a phenomenon which is both recognized and valued by teachers. A number of studies have

78

successfully operationalized the concept of teacher autonomy. A recent American study (Pearson and Hall, 1993), using a Teacher Autonomy Scale, provided strong support for the teaching autonomy construct. Studies using different research approaches (Jackson, 1968; Lortie, 1975; Nias, 1989) support the view that teachers are very conscious of their autonomy, which is an important factor in their sense of job satisfaction.

Although professional autonomy is in some instances subject to severe constraints, its persistence is made inevitable by the endemic uncertainties of teaching. The phrase 'endemic uncertainties, is Lortie's. In a chapter bearing that title, and elsewhere in his classic study *Schoolteacher* (Lortie, 1975), he explores the uncertainties inherent in what he terms the teacher's craft. He summarizes his position as follows: 'The teacher's craft, then, is marked by the absence of concrete models for evaluation, unclear lines of influence, multiple and controversial criteria, ambiguity about assessment, timing, and instability in the product' (p. 136).

The analysis offered in this chapter does not greatly differ from this. It takes account of developments in theory and practice since Lortie's work was published, and it is directly orientated (in a way in which Lortie's work was not, nor was intended to be) towards the issue of autonomy. In addition, although the discussion is concerned with the general issue of teacher autonomy, it will inevitably be shaped by the current situation in England and Wales.

Three areas of uncertainty will be considered: goals, school structure, and the classroom.

Uncertainties in the goals of education

The case for teacher autonomy would be weakened if the goals (or aims) of education could be stated with a high degree of precision in perennial and context-specific forms. If goals cannot be so specified, the role of the teacher lies in interpreting such different goals that are proclaimed and converting them into specific teaching tasks. Two points need to be made about these competing positions. One is that, to repeat an earlier more general point, neither position is tenable in its extreme form. There has never been, nor is there ever likely to be, a situation in which society leaves its teachers wholly free to determine their own goals and to convert these into more immediate teaching objectives. On the other hand, it is unlikely that any society would seek to control the work of teachers in every detail, or, if it did, it is unlikely that it could ensure compliance. The issue is again one of balance, and that balance will vary over space and time.

It will be the outcome of the efforts of the organized teaching profession, not necessarily to shape the goals of education, but to ensure that the goals established by governments do not greatly reduce the autonomy of the individual teacher. The tension between the two positions turns not only on the content, but on the very nature of educational goals and on what one might term the meta-goals of education, which we will consider first.

In the history of educational thought, again resorting to a necessary over-simplification, two positions on meta-goals have been advanced and defended. One sees the goal of education to be the pouring of a specific body of pre-existing knowledge into the empty vessel which is the pupil. The other sees the pupil as the active agent in his or her own learning, constructing, with the support of a teacher, personal resources of knowledge from available materials in accordance with needs and interests. This over-simplification is matched by the over-simplistic nature of the various labels which have been used to characterize these positions: traditional/progressive, subject-centred/child-centred, etc. These competing meta-goals generate different approaches to more substantive goals. Traditionalism favours predetermined and specific goals in terms of the bodies of knowledge and sets of skills which pupils are expected to learn, thus leading to detailed prescriptions as to curriculum content, teaching materials, pedagogic strategies and learning outcomes. This entails an educational time-scale which more or less ends with each stage of formal education, the pupil being considered as 'equipped' to move on to the next stage or into employment. The 'progressive' meta-goal, as its protagonists have frequently noted, sees the concept of education as a process, the nature of which is indicated by its Latin root of *educare*, in that it entails a drawing out. Thus curricula, materials and methods are seen as resources to be used in developing the individual. Goals are thus to be seen as emergent rather than prescribed, and the time-scale of the educative process is a lifetime. This perspective in its strongest form rejects the commodification of education and the equating of achievement and the acquisition of credentials. It is seen more as a process of learning how to learn.

Of course, these are over-simplified positions, two old war-horses which have pawed the ground before each other for gene-rations. The reality, as always, is at some point between the two extremes. Nevertheless, they continue to remain competing perspectives and to shape attitudes towards specific goals. Given the inescapable fact of a strong link between educational achievements and occupation in industrialized society, the con-tent goals of education, linked to credentials, have an appeal to consumers, and this is currently taken as the legitimation of a more prescriptive approach to educational goals – in a word, to the 'basics'. And the teacher's autonomy is thereby reduced. The aspiration of those who take this view is to be increasingly prescriptive in converting general goals into specific objectives. However, there are inherent limits to this. Unless those who hold this position are prepared to reduce education to training, they will always confront the dilemma which stems from the diverse and diffuse nature of educational goals.

Educational goals are diffuse because they are usually stated at such an order of generality that they are capable of a variety of interpretations. Though now somewhat historical, the fol-lowing list of goals exemplifies this diffuseness (DES, 1977a):

(1) to help children develop lively, inquiring minds; giving them the ability to question and argue rationally, and to apply themselves to tasks;

81

(2) to instil respect for moral values, for other people and for oneself, and tolerance of other races, religions, and ways of life;

(3) to help children understand the world in which we live, and the interdependence of nations;

(4) to help children to use language effectively and imaginatively in reading, writing and speaking;

(5) to help children to appreciate how the nation earns and maintains its standard of living and properly to esteem the essential role of industry and commerce in this process;

(6) to provide a basis of mathematical, scientific and technical knowledge, enabling boys and girls to learn the essential skills needed in a fast-changing world of work;

(7) to teach children about human achievement and aspirations in the arts and sciences, in religion, and in the search for a more just social order;

(8) to encourage and foster the development of the children whose social or environmental disadvantages cripple their capacity to learn, if necessary by making additional resources available to them. (pp. 6–7)

There is little in this list to which anyone could object as a set of educational goals which, if not perennial, are certainly relevant to late twentieth-century education in an industrialized society – though the fifth goal in the list betrays its time and its provenance and might well not have appeared in a similar list compiled a year or two earlier.

The list contains goals which are not only diffuse because they are expressed at a high level of abstraction, but also diverse in that they embrace not only knowledge and skills but also values, beliefs and attitudes, thus illustrating the general view that education is concerned with bringing about changes of quite a fundamental nature in people. Clearly such diffuse goals defy detailed specification in terms of curriculum objectives and teaching strategies. In the old cliché, these are 'caught' rather than 'taught', internalized through the informal curriculum and the climate of school and classroom, which are not easily prescribed. They may also be internalized through adopting the teacher as role model. Although some societies have sought to prescribe the values, attitudes, behaviour, dress and lesser activities appropriate to teachers, there are inherent limits to the degree that even the formal meeting of these expectations by teachers is effective in a democratic and post-modern society, let alone their internalization.

The goals in the list cited above would probably command the support of the vast majority of teachers. But this would not in any way reduce the autonomy of the teacher. There is probably little in the list which a teacher might wish not to implement, and the goals are sufficiently broad to cover most of the individual goals which a teacher might have. The problem is that these goals only give the broadest indication of what is to be taught. The list could be used to justify the broadest of aims, ranging from the elimination of sin to the attainment of cycling proficiency. The various goals compete for time, and although this difficulty can be partially resolved through a national curriculum which specifies the amount of time to be devoted to a particular subject and the components thereof, this cannot, other than through a *dirigisme* and a degree of supervision which would seem inoperable, obviate the necessity of according priorities as a matter of school policy and of classroom pedagogy. This is particularly true of those aspects of education which are not readily converted into specific curriculum components, which are currently referred to as cross-curricular themes and issues. And this applies *a fortiori* to the informal transmission of values.

Thus goals established for an education system can only partially reduce the endemic uncertainties of teaching. Even when they are given a degree of specificity in terms of a national curriculum and attainment targets, the scope for teachers' judgement and hence autonomy remains high. Within the broad framework set by a national curriculum, the operating goals are set at the level of the school and the classroom. Intermediate between the goals which are embodied in the school curriculum and classroom teaching styles and strategies is a set of professional requirements which are not appropriate areas of teacher autonomy in terms of whether or not they are carried out. These include lesson-planning, establishing routines which facilitate control, assessing pupils' work, etc. There is scope for autonomy in the way in which these tasks are carried out, but not in the matter of whether they are carried out or not.

Uncertainties in school structure

Schools are organizations and, like all organizations, exhibit the twin processes of *differentiation* and *co-ordination*. Differentiation entails a division of labour whereby teachers perform distinctive roles in relation to administration, teaching and pastoral care, and in terms of age-group or subject taught, etc. Co-ordination refers to those processes, largely managerial, which ensure the integration of these activities in relation to what are conventionally termed organizational goals. Differentiation creates scope for autonomy; co-ordination imposes constraints on autonomy. The tension between the two will be most obvious in those organizations, such as schools, universities and hospitals, which employ professionals. There is a substantial literature on the hypothesized bureaucratic–professional conflict (Davies, 1983). However, the conflict is not, in practice, quite as sharply experienced in schools as the theory sometimes suggests. The reason for this is that, as a matter of description – certainly until recent years – schools have been characterized as what has been termed *loosely coupled systems* (Weick, 1976), characterized by substantial *ambiguity* (March and Olsen, 1976), two works which have generated a substantial literature on the structural looseness of schools (see Tyler, 1988).

The fundamental characteristic of a loosely coupled system is that of an individual or group controlling and co-ordinating from the centre the activities of an organization which is structurally 'loose', i.e. the separate components – departments, teams and individual teachers – enjoy a relatively high degree of autonomy. The historical and functional reasons for the looseness are capable of a variety of interpretations, among which are values (i.e. a recognition of the fact that effective teaching is predicated on the relative autonomy of teachers as professionals), logistics (i.e. a recognition that teaching is not amenable to close control without substantial investment of resources in monitoring procedures), or micropolitical, (i.e. a stand-off whereby heads and teachers implicitly recognize the relative autonomy of the spheres of each party, which are, briefly, school policy in the case of the head and classroom pedagogy in the case of the teacher, with an intermediate area where the two spheres overlap and give rise to conflict, negotiation or micropolitics; Hanson, 1979).

This broad description of the main structural characteristics of the school as an organization indicates that there exists considerable scope for autonomy. Nevertheless, it would, perhaps be unwise to say that the relative autonomy is endemic, since, in theory, the structure of the school could be so bureaucratized that this autonomy would be lost as a result of more detailed specifications and tighter surveillance. However, although current trends are in the direction of greater control, and hence reduced autonomy, other aspects of schools as organizations suggest that there are inherent limitations to this. In particular, the extent of the ambiguity which exists in schools and the uncertain linkage between goals, structures, technology and outcomes.

The ambiguous nature of school goals arises from the diffuse and diverse nature of educational goals described above. The 'rational' model of organizations, which presents them as establishing specific goals, designing structures and procedures for the achievement of those goals and the evaluating of their effectiveness, has been widely criticized in the recent management literature. Although the classical management model may be effective in certain circumstances, e.g. where organizational activities can be routinized and environments are stable, many organizations are not of this kind. There are limits to the routinization of education. Moreover, organizations have various types of goal, of which 'output' goals, though undoubtedly important, are not the only form. The goals published by individual schools would seem to have a largely symbolic function. This is not to say that they are unimportant. They remind staff members of the ultimate purposes of the enterprise and constitute a cultural element which facilitates shared values, co-operation and a sense of belonging. However, they give only the very broadest guide to day-to-day operations. These stem from the specifications established by the head and/or management team, are negotiated collegially between management and teachers, or, importantly, emerge from the collaborative practices of teachers. With the current emphasis on school management, it is perhaps too easy to make assumptions about the strength of the linkage between management practices and pedagogical practices. One of the present authors has elsewhere (Hoyle, 1986) used the metaphor of an hourglass to convey the relationship between management and pedagogy: there is abundant activity in the upper (managerial) and lower (pedagogical) compartments, but the relationship between the two is unknown and may be slight. The relationship may well be changing as a result of the growth of quality assurance strategies and the school improvement movement, but one cannot say that the relationship has been considerably tightened or that it is inherently amenable to being further tightened.

It perhaps makes greater sense to see goals as emerging from activities rather than determining them. It also perhaps makes more sense to see organizational decisions emerging out of the interplay of a variety of factors than as the outcome of a linear process of identifying a problem, considering alternative solutions, selecting the most promising, implementing an action plan and evaluating the outcome. March and Olsen's famous 'garbage can' model holds that goals are the outcome of the interplay between solutions, participants, problems and choice opportunities. In this situation, which is a particular characteristic of educational organizations, March and Olsen (1976) summarize the situation as follows:

> The garbage can process, as it has been observed, is one in which problems, solutions and participants move from one choice opportunity to another in such a way that the nature of

the choice, the time it takes, and the problems it solves all
depend on a relatively complicated intermeshing of the mix of
choices available at any one time, the mix of problems that
have access to the organisation, the mix of solutions looking for
problems, and the outside demands on the decision makers.

(p. 36)

Since educational 'goals' are diffuse and diverse, they cannot
all be pursued with the same degree of commitment all the time.
Schools have to attend to a succession of goals. This is determined in part by external policies, so that the organizational
'energy' is focused upon whatever is given priority at the
national or local level: the National Curriculum, school
development plans, SATs, teacher appraisal, and so forth.
And apart from the predominant issue, commitment to the
other school issues, and to the perennial concerns of school –
discipline, relationships with parents, fund-raising, carol con-
certs and sponsored walk – ebb and flow according to seasonal
timing, resources, commitment, etc. 'Organized anarchy', as
March and Olsen (1976) term it, limits considerably the
possibility of tight central control and increases the scope for
teacher autonomy within the school as an organization. The
limits to control, and the potential for autonomy, are even
greater in that key pedagogical site – the classroom.

Uncertainties in the classroom

The complexity of the classroom as a social and as a learning
system is often overlooked, or deliberately over-simplified, by
those who aspire to a predictable relationship between a
specified pedagogy and a specified outcome. The 'class' is an
interplay between a set of pupils with diverse characteristics and
a teacher with a particular set of experiences, skills, values, etc.
which results in a distinctive style and set of pedagogic strategies, content to be transmitted and learned, and a range of
teaching resources. While there are undoubtedly some learning
drills which lead directly to the acquisition of specific skills or

87

facts and which may well be effectively deployed within a broader pedagogic strategy, for the most part neither the acquisition of knowledge nor the internalization of values, nor the development of interests, are achieved in this manner. All this is well known and attested by many decades of research on teaching and learning. Space does not allow an extensive review of this literature. Instead, under four general headings – equifinality, contingency, motivation, and culture – a number of observations can be offered which are supported by the literature and which confirm the endemic uncertainties of the classroom.

Equifinality

This term from systems theory indicates that the same result can be achieved by different sets of operations. In everyday language, 'There's more than one way of skinning a cat.' There may be instances in education where only one method can achieve the required result, but for the most part equifinality prevails. This is evidenced in the acquisition of those skills which are zero-sum: swimming, riding a bicycle, etc. The 'best' way of teaching these skills remains contested, and there are very different approaches to teaching, and manifestly the skills are acquired through a range of methods. Equifinality also applies to the techniques of mathematical manipulation, where teachers who 'swear by' the best method of teaching these and teachers who use different methods are, on all the evidence, equally effective. But, of course, most of what pupils learn in schools is not zero-sum, and achievements are relative and the effectiveness of teaching methods is thereby more difficult to evaluate. This is also true of some superficially zero-sum competences, in that although pupils might be able to apply a formula, there may be differences in their mathematical understanding of the formula. Thus the principle of equifinality means that methods cannot be rigidly tested in all situations. It is not, however, equifinality alone which determines the pedagogic uncertainties of the classroom, but equifinality in combination with the other factors discussed below.

Contingency

The contingent nature of teaching arises from the mix of variables which constitute the 'class' and the unpredictable dynamics of the mix. It must be stressed, however, that the classroom is not in a constant state of chaos – using this term in the sense of inherently low predictability, not in terms of the incompetence of the teacher – to the degree that there is no routine nor regular periods of ordered and predictable activities. Even in the most deliberately ordered classrooms (and there will be differences here according to individual teaching style, school climate and educational policies), in so far as classrooms are social systems they have the unpredictability which is present in all social interaction. In those societies which have emphasized active learning, one might expect classrooms to be even less predictable, and, in fact, naturalistic studies of classrooms in those societies have emphasized the qualities of immediacy, spontaneity, informality and individualism (Jackson, 1968).

In these situations, effective teaching is contingent teaching, a term here used to describe the capacity of teachers to adjust their styles and strategies to meet the needs of changing situations. This entails a constant adjustment between the polarities of formal/informal, didacticism/discovery, etc., while of course, retaining the integrity of the teaching role.

Research on the effectiveness of different styles and strategies is beset by conceptual and methodological problems and, despite the enormous literature on the topic, generalizations are hazardous. However, it is reasonably safe to make the generalization that effective teaching is neither, to use massively over-simplified terms by way of shorthand, formal nor informal, nor even a fixed balance between formal and informal, but a *moving* balance between the two styles. In other words, effective teaching entails a contingent mediation between the nature of the material and the characteristics of the learners.

Although contingency entails the adaptation of strategy to changing circumstances, it should not lead one to assume that there are no teaching strategies whatsoever which are generally accepted by experienced professionals. There are texts (e.g.

Kyriacou, 1986; Wragg, 1993) which, while recognizing the contingent nature of teaching, nevertheless identify strategies that have been found to be successful in most contexts. While teachers should retain sufficient autonomy to innovate and seek improvements if these strategies did not appear to be working well in a particular situation, it would seem, paradoxically perhaps, an intimation of a lack of professionality not to accept the weight of evidence and experience without good cause. Despite the essentially contingent nature of education, it would throw doubts upon teaching as a profession if it could lay claim to no general principles.

Motivation

The unpredictability of the classroom is also a function of the importance of teacher motivation in determining which teaching methods are appropriate. There is a well-known sociological adage which holds: 'When men (*sic*) define situations as real they are real in their consequence' (Thomas and Znaniecki, 1939). This could be adapted to read: 'If teachers define teaching methods as effective, they are effective in their consequence.' Of course, this is somewhat too over-simplified to be accepted as it stands. Not all teaching methods are likely to be equally effective, however much their protagonists believe in them. Moreover, there may well be moral objections to particular methods. If it could be demonstrated that pupils learned a mathematical technique more rapidly if they were smacked around the head whenever they made an error, there are likely to be only a few people who would condone that as a teaching strategy. Nevertheless, the linkage between belief, commitment and outcome is probably strong. One of the problems which bedevils research on teaching methods is the significance of the teacher-as-variable. It may well be that if human agency was removed certain teaching methods would technically be more effective than their alternatives, but it is very difficult to discount human agency. This is exemplified in the case of the teaching of reading. The common-sense view of the lay person might well be that different approaches to the teaching of reading could be ranked in terms of their effectiveness. This 'common sense' might be extended to encompass a view, without experience or evidence, on which of the various approaches was the most effective. However, the evidence is that teachers tend to adopt their own mix of strategies both in relation to the teaching of reading to all children and, within this overall strategy, in relation to the needs of particular children. It would therefore be extremely difficult, if not impossible, to identify the 'best' method of teaching reading. Although there is no necessary congruence between contingency and motivation, since a teacher may well believe that a single method of teaching is invariably effective, in practice such a relationship would appear to exist. Effective teachers who have sufficiently mastered the basic skills of classroom management to the degree to which they have the freedom and confidence to choose between methods, would seem to work out a set of strategies chosen from a range of possibilities and to believe in their effectiveness while at the same time modifying these according to experience, changing circumstances and continuing professional development.

Culture

We are here referring to *professional* culture, which connotes a related set of beliefs widely held within the teaching profession of England and Wales and, it would seem, other Anglo-Saxon countries. Such a culture shapes all aspects of the teacher's work, and although, for convenience, it is discussed here in the context of classroom teaching, it will be appreciated that it has wider implications. The term should not be taken as implying a high degree of consensus about curriculum and methods. This is not the case, and, in fact, it is a component of the meta-values of the professional culture that teachers should have a high degree of freedom in these areas, although the advent of the National Curriculum has limited the scope of such freedom. Three values can be suggested as constituting an important part of the culture of teaching.

Independence This element of the professional culture values the freedom of the individual teacher from the constraints of administrators, colleagues and lay people. It entails, in short, *autonomy*, but in its positive form it represents the freedom of the teacher to construct a personal pedagogy, which entails a balance between personality, training and experience and the requirements of a particular educational context. The value placed on independence is manifest in a number of research approaches. Studies of teacher satisfaction invariably show independence, autonomy or some similar notion is needed to be ranked very highly (see, e.g., Nias, 1989). Studies of teachers in the process of teaching also reveal their commitment to an independence which enables them to construct their own pedagogies and their own distinctive relationship with their classes. It is not, however, complete isolation and a total freedom to construct their own curricula that they want. As Jackson (1968) points out, the primary teachers in his US study wanted curriculum guidelines to be available should they choose to make use of them. They also wanted the support of their colleagues, but from outside their classrooms as it were.

There has been a strong norm of non-interference ingrained in the teaching profession. This is not only expressed in the reluctance of teachers to involve others in their professional activities, but also in the tendency to withhold from offering advice or suggesting intervention in some form. This has been particularly noticeable in the attitude of experienced teachers to neophytes. The norm in this country has been to allow new teachers to sink or swim rather than to intervene, except where massive problems of control are occurring; and despite the funding of development projects and avowals of intent, there is still relatively little intervention and not a great deal of support. However, this norm of non-interference is undergoing change in the direction of greater teacher collaboration. This will be discussed in further detail later in the present chapter.

Individualism Whereas the value of independence depicted above is the relative freedom of teachers from non-interference by other adults, individualism refers to the value accorded to the individual development of pupils. This is obviously related to the idea of *child-centred education*, a concept which has been the subject of considerable analysis for the best part of a century. A detailed conceptual analysis is beyond the scope of this chapter. It is perhaps sufficient to note that there is widespread commitment among teachers to the broad value of individualism. Education is seen more in terms of meeting the individual needs of children. Of course, as even the strongest protagonists of child-centred education allow, considerable constraints limit the possibility of full realization: the right of governments to see that social and economic requirements are met, the limitations imposed by the fact that pupils are taught in classes, etc. Nevertheless, in so far as individualism is a widely held value in education, it is predicated upon the teacher having a sufficient degree of autonomy to make judgements in the interest of the needs of individual pupils.

Pragmatism This term is not deployed in this context with any philosophical precision. It is used broadly to connote a widespread commitment by teachers to the practical, what appears to work, in the teaching–learning process. Teachers' antipathy to 'theory' is well-documented, though this resistance is not uniform towards all forms of theory. For example, Lortie (1975) points out that teachers are particularly resistant to theories of teaching which appear to them to be impractical and, in some instances, utopian. The use which teachers make of 'theory' is a complex issue which has been discussed in sone detail in Chapter 3. Teachers rely heavily on experience and the practical guidelines given during initial and in-service training.

In so far as they incorporate theory into their daily practices, it is not monolithic, but derived from a variety of sources in accordance with its congruence with the immediate practicalities of the classroom. This essentially pragmatic approach requires a high degree of autonomy, since the pragmatic approach requires the freedom to make context-bound decisions.

93

Autonomy and collaboration

A model of professional autonomy based on the notion of an independent practitioner is inappropriate when applied to professionals who work in organizations. One reason is that organizational constraints inevitably limit autonomy. Another is that professional collaboration, which inevitably reduces the autonomy of the individual practitioner, is generally held to provide a more effective service. There is a growing body of work which suggests that the quality of education is enhanced when teachers work more closely together. An additional case for professional collaboration holds that professionals should collaborate in formulating the policies which will shape their activities at the organizational level.

Teacher collaboration has been an issue for thirty years, but the degree and the manner in which it has been implemented has been uncertain and has varied with the political climate. It initially became an issue in the 1960s and was given an impetus both by socio-political and by educational change. A key notion in the political culture of the time was that of *participation*, the belief that those who would be affected by decisions should participate in making them. In education this was held to entail the participation not only of staff but also of students. The problem was that the participation of teachers in decision-making was not specifically supported by central government, which was still in a *laissez-faire* mode in relation to education. Nor was the legal authority of the headteacher modified to allow for the formal sharing of responsibility. Nevertheless, many heads, on their own initiative or under pressure from staff, sought to establish structures for participation, varying from increased consultation to the devolution of decision-making to groups of staff. Because these changes were more a function of management style rather than of changed patterns of governance, no uniform pattern emerged and, despite the changes, the loosely coupled structure of the school and relative independence of policy/planning functions and pedagogy remained relatively intact. Nevertheless, the participation of staff in decision-making was a growing feature of schools during the period between the early 1960s and the mid-1970s. With the changing political climate of the late 1970s and 1980s the issue of participation ceased to be quite so salient, but in the later 1980s and early 1990s the issue re-emerged, though with a somewhat different ideological weighting. The dual strategy of centralization and decentralization, and the marginalization of Local Education Authorities, put a premium on the decision-making capacities of the school. The power of the governors and the head was increased, which, to some extent, militated against decision-making as a collaborative professional enterprise, but the participation of teachers in policy and planning – for example in the formulation of institutional development plans and other school-wide activities – was encouraged, and for the first time headteachers were legally required to consult other members of staff by the Education Act of 1991. Thus collaborative professionality is a current policy in education, but the implications for teacher autonomy are still unclear, and the issue will be considered below.

The second source of pressure towards teacher collaboration in the 1960s arose from, and to some extent was integral to, changes in curriculum, pedagogy and assessment. There was a movement during that period in the following directions: interdisciplinary enquiry, discovery learning, flexible timetabling, resource-based learning, mixed-ability grouping, open-plan architecture, etc.

A general feature of these innovations was a weakening of boundaries between subjects, teacher and taught, categories of pupils, timetable divisions, teaching groups, school and community, and physical space in the school. These changes were predicated upon a much greater degree of professional collaboration between teachers, since, as Bernstein, who wrote with great weight on these changes, put it, 'teachers will no longer step into assigned duties. Their roles will no longer be made but will have to be made' (Bernstein, 1975, p. 171). Thus the changes were predicated not upon a reduction in the independence and isolation of teachers, but on their collaboration.

They assumed a reduction in the strength of the boundary between teacher roles at the levels of policy, planning and, particularly in the case of team-teaching, in pedagogy.

These changes in curriculum and pedagogy were perhaps more discussed than implemented, and although many schools moved to some extent in the direction indicated, there occurred no fundamental and lasting shift. However, three suggestions can be made as to why this was the case. One is that the implementation of these curriculum changes was essentially a matter for the school, and although the elements of a strategy for school-based change had been hypothesized, they had not been widely implemented and thus innovation foundered for the lack of a collaborative professional strategy and individual teachers began to experience innovation fatigue. Another is that the innovations either had or, more often, had attributed to them an ideological loading which rendered them unacceptable to educational stakeholders. The furore surrounding the William Tyndale Infant and Junior School exemplified this (Auld, 1976). These attitudes were reflected initially in the Ruskin Speech of 1976 and were given much stronger expression in words and policies following the election of the Conservative government in 1979.

Thus the curriculum changes of the 1960s and early 1970s were either taken no further or reversed in the two following decades, and there was consequently little further development in modes of professional collaboration. These were in any case overtaken by the increasing focus on the management of schools during this period. In so far as the curriculum innovations of the 1960s were continued in the 1980s, they were confined to the programmes funded under the TVEI scheme, which involved professional collaboration not only within but also between schools. Otherwise a major difference between the 1960s–1970s and the 1980s–1990s was that, whereas in the earlier period the curriculum was a school concern, in the later period a national curriculum had been imposed on schools. However, there is a considerable irony in the fact that some of the strategies proposed in the 1960s and early 1970s for professional collaboration for curricular and pedagogical innovation are now being sponsored by central government, but now as a contrivance to ensure that promulgated change is effectively implemented.

There is little doubt that the quality of education is enhanced when teachers work more closely together. A growing body of literature on school improvement and effectiveness almost universally reports the beneficial effects of this collaboration, e.g. Fullan (1991; 1993), Hargreaves and Hopkins (1991), Nias *et al.* (1989). This is undoubtedly the most promising future direction for teacher professionality. However, we have in play a variety of terms to describe the relevant process(es): *collegial, collaborative, participative, integrative*, which may each be linked to such terms as *culture* and *climate* and *professionality* and *professionalism*. The terms may or may not be referring to the same phenomenon. They can be defined differently and operationalized differently. At the level of semantics this does not matter, and the writers cited above are all very experienced researchers who make clear in each case the empirical referent of their terms. But, in the wider debate, there may well be confusion abroad, and there is a danger of unwarranted enthusiasm – mostly – but also of unwarranted pessimism.

One needs to be clear about the *areas* of involvement, perhaps drawing a crude distinction between *policy, planning* and *pedagogy*, since it would appear that, while teachers are becoming increasingly collaborative at the levels of policy and planning, this is less obvious and perhaps less achievable at the level of pedagogy. One also needs to know the degree to which collaboration is *voluntary, enforced* (Smyth, 1991), or *contrived* (Hargreaves and Dawe, 1990). And one needs to know the degree to which collaboration emerges from the *culture* or *climate* of a school or is incorporated in its *structure*. Many other distinctions could be made. The task of clarifying the terminology and, more importantly, mapping the practices to which they relate has yet to be undertaken, and one must therefore be content with making a number of points.

In a paper which is highly relevant to the present discussion,

Little (1990) suggests that collaboration can be ranged on a continuum from *independence* to *interdependence*, which has ranged along it a set of discrete activities which include storytelling and scanning, aid and assistance, sharing and joint work (i.e. 'the shared responsibility for the work of teaching'). She is not wholly sanguine about some of the claims made for collaboration. She writes:

> When I attend closely to the accounts of teachers' professional relationships that have accumulated over the past decade, however, I am confronted by certain inescapable conclusions. A few schools stand out for the achievements wrought collectively by their faculties but much 'that passes for collegiality does not add up to much'. Teachers' collaborations sometimes serve the purposes of well-conceived change, but the assumed link between increased collegial contact and improvement-oriented change does not seem to be warranted: closely bound groups are instruments both for promoting change and for conserving the present. Changes, indeed, may prove substantial or trivial. Finally, collaborations may arise naturally out of the problems and circumstances that teachers experience in common, but often they appear contrived, inauthentic, grafted on, perched precariously (and often temporarily) on the margins of real work.   (pp. 507–8)

The rhetoric of collegiality sometimes ignores the distribution of power in the school (Ball, 1992). There is a *strong* and a *weak* connotation of collegiality. A strong connotation was offered by Lortie (1964) when he described collegiality as 'a situation in which professional equals govern their affairs through democratic procedures' (p. 283). A weak connotation would equate with a looser form of voluntary collaboration. The 'strong' connotation implies that authority rests with the collegial group. This is not the case in England and Wales. Heads have authority, teachers have influence. It is one of the key tasks of headship to establish structures whereby teachers make their professional input to policy-making. One must therefore place collegiality within the substantial literature on patterns of participation which has been most recently reviewed by Bacharach *et al.* (1990). Teachers vary in their desire for participation in general and in the specific areas of decision-making in which they wish to participate. Satisfaction is a function of the relationship between a wish to participate and the opportunity to do so.

The literature suggests that the most effective professional collaboration occurs where the culture or climate of the school supports it. Collaborative professionality is used here to describe a pattern of professional collaboration among teachers which is emergent, voluntaristic, and related to specific pedagogical problems. It is a cultural rather than a structural dimension of schools, although its patterns may become institutionalized. Hargreaves and Dawe (1990) define collaborative cultures as comprising 'evolutionary relationships of openness, trust and support among teachers where they define and develop their own purposes as a community' (p. 239). An excellent study of collaborative cultures by Nias *et al.* (1989) describes a collaborative culture as follows:

> To sum up, the 'culture of collaboration' arises from and embodies a set of what may broadly be described as moral beliefs about the value of the relationship between individuals and groups. It does not grow from shared beliefs about the nature or organization of curriculum content or teaching methods, but it has an impact in several ways upon educational practice in a school. It leads over time to the formation of a broad curricular and pedagogical consensus, tolerant of difference and divergence. It is an instrument of social and moral education, through the hidden curriculum and especially through the attitude and behaviour of staff towards one another. It encourages a sense of team pride and so of hard work, and it facilitates relaxed, spontaneous co-operation over teaching and other professional responsibilities. (p. 53)

The collaborative culture is located in interpersonal relationships rather than educational beliefs. The writers recognize that teachers bring into schools beliefs from their own subcultures, whether 'infant' or 'junior' – and in secondary schools, of course, there are strong subject subcultures. Teachers also differ in their views of pedagogy. However, although the culture of collaboration was found to be primarily concerned with personal relationships rather than pedagogy, these writers suggest it had an indirect effect upon educational practice. There were some broad areas of agreement and the heads had established a mission for their schools. Individuality was respected, although those with extreme educational views were marginalized.

It remains an interesting question as to whether this culture arose because collaboration formed no part of a clear centralized strategy. Hargreaves (1992) has recently written of it as follows:

> Collaboration cannot be legislated into existence to replace
> individualism any more than virtue can be legislated to
> supersede vice. But we must not jump to a romantic, and very
> unsociological, position which assumes that collegiality springs
> up 'naturally' and 'spontaneously' when teachers are free from
> political and administrative intrusions. Collaboration is a
> culture that grows from structural roots, and these are indeed, .
> as I have argued, affected by legislation and imposed reform.
>
> (p. 6)

The collaborative culture described by Nias and her colleagues was grounded in a pattern of interaction rather than a shared body of professional knowledge – though this element was not wholly absent. It is unlikely that teaching will ever reach the stage of having a culture based on an agreed body of knowledge. This is not to say that a substantial body of educational research has not been built up over the years, but no one supposes that one can 'read off' direct implications for practice. Teachers construct the knowledge base which underpins practice from a variety of sources: experience, colleagues *and* the literature. Professionality will be enhanced to the degree that learning from colleagues and the literature is increased. It would seem that the best way forward lies in strengthening the interpersonal element in the professional culture as described by Nias *et al.* (1989) and others. However, this culture will be strengthened to the degree that the discourse transcended immediate concerns. This is where Schon's well-known concept of the reflective practitioner (Schon, 1987) becomes relevant. It is the reflection on practice which might constitute an increasingly important component of professional discourse, and it is perhaps the defence of one's professional practice which constitutes the essence of appraisal. Aspects of professionality and reflectiveness will be discussed further in Chapter 5.

Conclusion

The traditional model of the professional enjoying a high degree of autonomy no longer holds. There has recently been a growing trend to introduce accountability measures in relation to all the professions, and these limit, as they are designed to do, the autonomy of the individual practitioner. The model is also inappropriate in the case of those professions, such as teaching, whose members work in organizations. The imperatives of co-ordination serve to limit individual autonomy in the interests of the collective purposes of the organization. Although effective education remains largely a function of the competence of individual teachers, research on schools shows the importance of the school factor in effectiveness, suggesting the importance of the collaborative effects of teaching.

Yet there are limits to the degree to which autonomy can, or should, be reduced, either through accountability measures or through misplaced efforts to achieve collegiality. There is a considerable degree of uncertainty and ambiguity inherent in the educational enterprise, due to the diverse and diffuse nature of educational goals, the contingent nature of classrooms, and the principle of equifinality. Moreover, autonomy and job satisfaction are closely linked, and it is very likely that satisfaction enhances effectiveness. While it is the case that the integration of teachers' activities within the structure of the school is important, it would appear that a contingent balance between control and autonomy, which is inherent in the nature of the school as a loosely coupled system, continues to offer the best scope for maximizing the professionality of teachers.

The key task at the present time is to develop collaborative patterns of professionality in which the strengths of teachers in a particular school are mobilized without undermining individual autonomy to a point which has a deleterious effect on teacher motivation and hence effectiveness. These collaborative patterns can be structured, but such evidence that we have suggests that effective collaboration is more a matter of climate, particularly a climate which optimizes collaboration while allowing for differences between teachers. Achieving this difficult feat of creating such a climate is a central task for the headteacher, but the leadership skill by which this is achieved is an aspect of another kind of professionality but a kind which is beyond the scope of this book.

5 The issue of responsibility

The argument of this chapter is underpinned by the assumption that although members of the professions have no monopoly on responsible behaviour, responsibility towards clients is an essential component of the idea of a profession. Responsibility is the reciprocal of autonomy. In so far as the professions enjoy autonomy (and the case for the inevitability of teacher autonomy has been made in the preceding chapter), it must be assumed that the freedom which this allows the practitioner must be exercised responsibly. This means that the practitioner's actions must ultimately be guided by a set of values which place a premium on client interests. it is unrealistic to assume that client interests would be invariably paramount. There are some for whom teaching is a *calling*, but for the majority it is a *career* in the narrower sense of personal advancement within the occupational hierarchy and in the wider sense of how a person manages his or her life. Professional commitment is a part of this life, and, though its intensity is variable, any teacher who acts professionally will not be untouched by it. But the management of a life also entails a commitment to a lifestyle and the acquisition of the leisure and the resources through and with which it is maintained. Thus, although the idea of a profession cannot realistically entail a total commitment to the priority of client interests, the ideal cannot be, and should not be, wholly absent. Responsibility entails an appropriate balancing of personal interests and client interests.

For the purpose of the argument in this chapter, *responsibility* is given a different connotation from *accountability*. It is conceptualized as being a broader principle. To accept the need for,

103

and to respond to, the processes of accountability is to be responsible. In general terms, accountability entails meeting the requirements of a set of procedures designed to assure the various clients of a profession that the accounting units (e.g. individual teachers, departments, schools, etc.) are meeting appropriate standards of practice. Responsibility entails a more voluntaristic commitment to a set of principles governing good practice, and the realization of these through day-to-day professional activities. These principles include *inter alia* the recognition of and compliance with the requirements of accountability, but responsibility reaches the parts which accountability cannot always reach since they are more fundamental. And, because they are more fundamental, at times they could be in conflict with governmental requirements of accountability. A recent example of this occurred in 1993 when the teaching profession as a whole, mobilized by all the teacher associations, resisted the government's programme of pupil testing, an accountability measure, on the grounds that it was inimical to effective education. It was a position which was upheld by the courts, and, despite government pressure, the testing did not go ahead.

This distinction between responsibility and accountability has been made in similar, though not identical, terms elsewhere. Pateman (1978) quotes Warnock (1977) as contrasting 'the accountability of an institution to another institution, with legal or quasi-legal authority over it, which an institution may owe or feel it owes to those it affects: but where those affected do not, directly, exercise authority over it' (p. 61). Pateman quite rightly notes, however, that in the real world responsibility and accountability are so intimately interrelated that it is difficult always to distinguish between the operation of the two principles. This is undoubtedly so, but it is useful to continue to draw a distinction at a theoretical level since, at the present time in particular, there is perhaps an implicit assumption within government that accountability and responsibility are synonymous. We can therefore consider the principles and practice of accountability before considering responsibility.

Accountability

Accountability is a term which suggests a businesslike precision. This is perhaps because, as a word, it shares a common root with accountancy, which in turn, through semantic association, suggests the notion of accuracy. (This idea of precision has perhaps been somewhat diluted in recent years with the practice of 'creative accounting'. It may well be that this has its analogue in what one might call 'creative accountability' – but that's another story!) Despite its apparent precision, accountability is a somewhat baggy concept, which Maclure (1978) has referred to as a metaphor. The basic questions to be asked when seeking to understand accountability are: Who is to be accountable? to whom? for what? and how? The answers to these questions could constitute a model of accountability which included an integrated set of procedures. However, there is little point, at least in this context, in constructing an abstract systematic model. The elements which might go into such a model are expertly discussed in the various contributions to Becher and Maclure (1978), though no single, prescriptive model is offered. The point is that accountability measures in education have not been derived from a systematic management model, but have been swept in on successive waves of government initiatives, mainly intended to tackle in an *ad hoc* way perceived shortcomings in the educational system.

Before what might be termed the accountability movement, which was initiated by Callaghan's Ruskin Speech of 1976, the accountability of teachers for their professional activities had been a somewhat hit and miss affair. Teachers were, of course, subject to the law and could be prosecuted for any illegal activities in which they engaged in the course of their professional duties, which were usually violence or sexual abuse or financial irregularities. They could also be dismissed following due process. Dismissals tended, again, to be largely for reasons of violence, sexual abuse, alcoholism, chronic absenteeism, and so forth. Teachers could also be dismissed for professional incompetence, though this was rare and was usually occasioned

105

by complete inability to control pupils. If a teacher could maintain control, the chances of dismissal for ineffective teaching were somewhat remote. In the absence of a self-governing professional body, the arbiter in dismissal cases was the employing authority, which had to have a case which was defensible in a court of law. Since ineffective teaching implies a clear criterion of effective teaching, and since such a criterion is not easily formulated at a level which would meet legal requirements of evidence, relatively few cases reached the courts.

Modes of accountability before 1976 embraced a very loosely related set of procedures and processes. Procedures, using this form to refer to formal explicit and systematic forms of assessment and reporting, were relatively few. At the secondary level, achievements in external examinations constituted the data most obviously in the public domain. The processes of assessment centred largely on the monitoring activities of the head-teacher, sometimes with heads of departments as intermediaries. The extent and depth of this monitoring remained largely a function of the leadership style of the headteacher. However, 'heavy' monitoring was contrary to the prevailing norm of autonomy. Teachers were exposed to informal peer pressures in relation to their classroom competence, but there was little or no systematic peer appraisal, and the strong norms of autonomy and independence inhibited the involvement of one teacher in the work of another.

As there were very few prescriptions, set down by central government, relating to the curriculum, and virtually none relating to pedagogy, headteachers' monitoring activities were guided by their professional judgement. HMI inspections and visits provided some professional guidance relating to curriculum and pedagogy, and, very occasionally, included informal advice relating to individual teachers. But inspections were infrequent, visits few, and observations of teachers, even teachers in their probationary year, rare. More influential, perhaps, in relation to the accountability of heads, departments and individual teachers were LEA inspectors and advisers, whose visits were more frequent than those of HMI. Teachers had relatively little direct accountability to parents. Contacts were mainly fleeting and informal, with only a five-minute discussion at the annual parents' evening constituting any semblance of formal interaction, and these, of course, were meetings for report rather than for account, since few parents questioned the teacher closely on curricular or pedagogical issues. Again, the head was the central figure. Parents with queries or concerns addressed these to the head rather than to the individual teacher. The head was also the person who interacted directly with external groups and individuals who had some sort of stake in the activities of schools. Finally, although managers and governors had some powers which might have enabled them to exercise some accountability, they seldom did so, and were heavily 'guided' by the head in their discussions. In fact, the establishment of the Taylor Committee (DES, 1977b) on the role of governors was one of the first initiatives in the accountability movement.

The above brief and necessarily over-simplified impression of the processes at work before the onset of the accountability movement perhaps, as stated, conveys a somewhat *laissez-faire* and unaccountable teaching profession. This is certainly the view which has been used to legitimize the accountability procedures which have been subsequently established. However, this is only one perspective. Another view is that, in the terms as used in this discussion, teachers may have been largely unaccountable, but they have not been irresponsible. It could be argued that their relative autonomy was matched by a generally high level of professional integrity and responsibility. It would be very difficult to demonstrate this as a fact, just as it would be difficult to demonstrate that an absence of accountability had led to very low professional standards. Without compelling evidence on either side, the dispute between the protagonists of the competing positions is futile. However, because of the prevailing view that lack of accountability *was* accompanied by low professional standards, it is at least worthwhile to point out that a different interpretation is just as tenable, given the absence of conclusive evidence either way.

The accountability movement consisted of an accelerating introduction of diverse measures which arose from a New Right political ideology and which gave rise to a general strategy for increasing the accountability of all the professions. In relation to education, at least, there was no consistent, integrated strategy, but largely a set of very loosely related measures. These involved both an increase in central powers and a devolution of some responsibilities to schools. A somewhat *ad hoc* list of some of the plethora of measures taken to ensure accountability is as follows:

Increased powers for governors.
Local management of schools.
Grant maintained status.
Open enrolment.
The National Curriculum.
Standard attainment tests.
Systematic inspection by OFSTED-approved teams.
Publication of inspection reports.
Institutional development plans.
Publication of examination results and other data.
Teacher appraisal.

These measures are diverse in terms of the matters for which the teaching profession is to be held accountable, the unit of account (e.g. teacher, school), the data on which accountability is to be based, the groups to whom teachers are accountable, the regularity and timing of the accounts, etc. If we accept Darling-Hammond's distinction between different forms of accountability, we can see the general pattern. The following are the five most relevant patterns as identified by Darling-Hammond (1989):

political accountability – elected officials must stand for
re-election at regular intervals so that citizens can judge the
representativeness of their views and the responsiveness of their
decisions;

legal accountability – courts must entertain complaints about violations of laws enacted by representatives of the public and of citizens' constitutionally granted rights, which may be threatened either by private or by legislative action;

bureaucratic accountability – agencies of government promulgate rules and regulations intended to assure citizens that public functions will be carried out in pursuit of public goals voiced through democratic or legal processes;

professional accountability – governments may create professional bodies and structures to ensure competence and appropriate practice in occupations that serve the public and may delegate certain decisions about occupational membership, standards, and practices to these bodies;

market accountability – governments may choose to allow clients or consumers to choose what services best meet their needs; to preserve the utility of this form of accountability, monopolies are prevented, freedom of choice is protected, and truthful information is required of service providers. (p. 61)

In broad terms, the accountability movement has adopted a mixture of bureaucratic and market forms. As conceptualized by Darling-Hammond, professional accountability embraces formal accountability through professional bodies. The accountability movement has not led to the establishment of such bodies, and although the profession itself has created a General Teaching Council as an incorporated body, it has not been formally recognized by government and hence has had no role to play in the accountability process. However, the concept of professional accountability can be both enlarged and sub-divided beyond Darling-Hammond's formulation. Perhaps three dimensions can be broadly distinguished. One corres-ponds to Darling-Hammond's formulation, i.e. accountability to professional bodies. Another is the informal professional accountability whereby professionals recognize and act upon a duty to clients – which in this chapter we refer to as respon-sibility. An intermediate position is one where professionals are collectively responsible for monitoring and reporting on the quality of professional practice.

In so far as the accountability movement has embraced a

professional component, it has taken the latter form. This is, perhaps, revealed in a growing emphasis on quality assurance. This is essentially, of course, a mode of accountability, and many of the methods of quality assurance involve the sort of reporting which is entailed in accountability. But a distinctive feature is that quality assurance depends, in part, upon professional collaboration, not only in ensuring quality, but in having an open and positive commitment to reporting the achievement, or otherwise, of quality outcomes.

Accountability is not in principle inimical to the idea of a profession. It may be that some patterns of accountability, for example those which are excessively bureaucratic or rely largely on the market, may serve to undermine the professions as currently conceived, but patterns in which the professions play an important, if no longer a dominant, role in formulating procedures are appropriate to a democracy. The challenge is to sustain, through a process of continuous negotiation between professions and the state, the *via media*. Shulman (1983) has written: 'We must somehow find a way to make teaching and systems of education simultaneously both responsible and free' (p. 497). In the terms adopted in this chapter, one can adapt that statement to read: We must somehow find a way to make teaching and systems of education both responsible and accountable. Systems of accountability are vital to the attainment of quality education, but they are not in themselves sufficient. They must be balanced by responsibility. The distinction must be sustained in any negotiations between representatives of the teaching profession and the government.

Responsibility

The nature of responsibility is a philosophical question of some magnitude. However, it is beyond the scope of this book, and the competence of its authors, to unpack this concept in a philosophically sophisticated manner. In his discussion of conceptions of responsibility in the context of a consideration of teaching as a profession, Langford (1985) makes a distinction which is central to our purpose here between *agent-for-another* and *principal*. He writes:

> An agent for another, if he is a responsible person, accepts responsibility for achieving the ends or purpose towards which his actions are directed; but the only purpose of his own which is involved in what he does is his desire to make a living. A principal, on the other hand, is responsible not merely for achieving but also for setting the ends of his actions; it is his purposes which are reflected in what he does and not merely those of others. It need not follow, of course, that his purposes are not shared by other members of the same profession or of the community to which that profession belongs. (p. 55)

This distinction is useful in considering the difference between accountability and responsibility.

Accountability is predicated upon the teacher as agent-for-another. The 'other' is, to put it in the singular for the moment, the client. The individual teacher, or the collectivity of teachers, is accountable to clients for the actions they take in the interests of those clients, and accountability procedures are the means by which they act as agents are guaranteed. Responsibility, on the other hand, is predicated upon the teacher acting as principal.

In the accountability–responsibility relationship there are areas of professional practice where accountability stands alone. In others, areas – the majority – responsibility and accountability are related but responsibility is exercised prior to accountability. And there are areas in which responsibility stands alone.

Accountability would stand alone where practice is pre-ordained as relatively routine. The teacher is acting here as agent, and professionality entails efficient delivery of a particular requirement. Responsibility is prior to accountability in many aspects of the teacher's work. This follows from our argument about the inherent diversity of goals and equifinality of pedagogy. In these areas the teacher has to make decisions as principal and exercise judgement. Teachers are inevitably doing

111

this in the course of their daily activities in classroom, school and beyond. Teachers are potentially accountable for these decisions *post factum*, and their accountability will take the form of a justification to the headteacher, governors, parents, inspectors, etc., of their outcomes, which may be in the form of products (e.g. test or exam results) or processes (e.g. teaching styles). This would also be true of teachers collectively, e.g. a school staff.

Being accountable entails being responsible. Accountability is a component of professional responsibility. However, although the account may be made in terms determined by the representatives of clients, (e.g. test scores), the accounts will often be in terms determined by the professionals themselves, which entails a double responsibility. Responsibility may well also be exercised independently of accountability. This comes about because, without a costly, draconian and ultimately self-defeating set of surveillance and reporting procedures, much of the teacher's work is beyond the scope of accountability. This is, perhaps, a somewhat negative dimension of responsibility, but it is, nevertheless, important. Teachers must be expected to be responsible even when the chances of being held to account are slim.

Thus, responsibility encompasses but transcends accountability because choice and judgement are necessary. They can be equated only if accountability is in large measure collegial accountability, and if this is seen much more in terms of culture than structure and procedure. If the above argument for a conceptual distinction to be drawn between responsibility and accountability has any merit, it is clear that responsibility cannot be wholly pre-ordained. The argument that the endemic uncertainties of education put a premium on autonomy is relevant to the issue of responsibility. Responsibility is essentially contingent because it entails making judgements in uncertain and changing situations and resolving conflicts by making a choice in one direction rather than another. Any *post factum* accountability must take into account this contingency.

In order to illustrate the contingent context in which responsibility and accountability occur, we will first explore, aspects of the professional role of the teacher, and then the characteristics of their clientele.

The role of the teacher

Teacher is an occupational role, the nature of which is relatively unequivocal in Britain. By and large, Qualified Teacher Status bestows a licence to practise on teachers, although it is the case that a greater proportion of teachers in the independent sector than in the state sector do not have QTS. Qualified teachers have certain conditions of employment which are legally sanctioned and constitute a form of accountability. However, our concern here is less with legal requirements than with the *expectations* which various social groups hold of the role of the teacher. In this respect, the teacher's role differs from many other occupational roles in terms of the range of groups which have specific expectations of the teacher's role and the range of expectations which they hold.

The *role set* of the teacher includes at least thirty categories. Some of the most obvious are pupils, professional colleagues, parents, governors, inspectors, politicians, employers, publishers, and the many groups which would like to see material relevant to their interests furthered by being included in the curriculum or otherwise dealt with by teachers. These components of the role set can be distinguished in at least two ways – the degree of direct contact with teachers and the degree of power inherent in their expectations. Clearly pupils and colleagues have the most sustained direct contact with the individual teacher, whereas governors, inspectors and elected members of national and local governments have the greatest power. If one distinguishes between two forms of power – *authority* and *influence* (Bacharach and Lawler, 1980), most of the teacher's face-to-face contacts have influence rather than authority, and their expectations might be expected to be effective in so far as the various modes of influence – personality,

113

expertise, etc. – are effective. The exception here lies within the professional subset, since the headteacher has access to resources of both influence and authority, and this combination is particularly salient. The government, though distant from the teacher, has the authority to give legal force to expectations.

The diffuse and diverse nature of educational goals has as its counterpart the expectations attached to the roles of teachers. These expectations relate to the qualities of the teacher as a person, teaching styles and strategies, the content of what they teach, the measures they take to maintain or improve their competence, and so forth. Many lists of the elements of the teacher's role which can be the basis of expectations have been constructed. A list which includes curricular and pedagogical elements is offered by Macdonald (1970) in a somewhat ironic manner, listing the characteristics of the 'omnicapable' teacher:

> Teachers are invited to refer themselves to an omnicapable model, at once intelligent and affectively warm, knowledgeable and tolerant, articulate and patient, efficient and gentle, morally committed and sympathetic, scholarly and practical, socially conscious and dedicated to personal development, fearless and responsible. They are told that they must be specialists in an academic discipline, masters of the techniques of presentation, adept class managers, artful motivators, skilful diagnosticians, ingenious remedial workers, imaginative curriculum designers, eager enquirers, efficient administrators, helpful colleagues, widely interested citizens, and loving human beings (the last being a new and very modish injunction). This rush of adjectives, so much in play when educators talk about teaching, can be summarized in a single phrase: teachers are, or ought to be, secular priests. (p. 16)

In Britain it has long been expected that the teacher's role would be much wider than simply the transmission of knowledge and skills. It is expected that they have developmental as well as didactic, socializing as well as academic, concerns. This has been revealed in a study of perceptions of the professional responsibilities of primary school teachers in France and in

England and Wales, where the following differences have been observed (Broadfoot and Osborn, 1988):

Teachers in England	Teachers in France
1. Define what is to be learned in terms of pupil needs interests.	Transmit a specific body of knowledge as 'cultural capital'.
2. Teaching style problematic because of pupil needs and external expectations.	Unproblematic pedagogy.
3. Uncertainty about professional goals because of expectations of competing groups.	Impermeable to dictates other than those of central government and accept an educational philosophy which is essentially traditional.
4. Accept responsibility for social and personal outcomes of schooling.	Accept responsibility only for academic outcomes of schooling.
5. Look to colleagues for moral support on their professional views of pupils.	Function independently of other teachers in determining their views of pupils.
6. Covert evaluation of pupils.	Overt evaluation of pupils via regular assessment of achievement.

It will be noted from the above that teachers in France apparently attend only to the expectations of a limited number of components of their role set.

In the past twenty-five years or so there has been an expansion, indeed an explosion, of the expectations attaching to the role of the teacher in England and Wales – and a response to those expectations which has lead perhaps to the point of role overload. The following are some of the areas in which expectations have increased:

Curriculum development.
School management.
Examination and assessment.
Educational technology.
Links with the social services.
Responsiveness to parents.
Pastoral care.
Personal and social education.
Combating racism and sexism.
Professional development.

There are several points to be made about this range of expectations, in addition to the fact that they vary in their provenance and in the weight of authority which they separately carry.

One is that, just as the goals of education cannot be fully achieved, so the expectations placed on the teacher cannot be met in full, and in some instances where they might in principle be met, it is difficult (if not impossible) to establish the degree to which this has occurred. This applies particularly to the expectation that teachers will bring about non-cognitive changes in pupils in relation, say, to their social and moral behaviour, and also applies to the long-term effects of teaching. In any case, such changes and effects, where they occur, are more likely to be the result of the efforts of a number of teachers.

Second, the expectations attaching to the teacher's role are so extensive that one could say that a teacher's work is never done. There is potentially no end to the time which teachers might spend out of school hours in preparation, marking, and attending meetings, courses and conferences, etc., which would enhance the quality of the education they provide. But, unless the teacher is to neglect expectations attaching to other roles (e.g. family), limitations have to be placed on these activities.

Third, even within school hours, teachers have to be selective in the expectations which they attempt to meet. They have to give priority to some rather than others, change priorities when they judge it appropriate, and, in relation to any particular expectation, determine the degree of commitment which they make.

Fourth, teachers have to resolve on a continuing basis the conflicts which arise because of differences in expectations. As with educational goals, some expectations are inherently incompatible. The potential conflict between expectations has increased in recent years because of three major factors. One is that as governments have become much more directly involved in education, expectations have become more prescriptive and detailed and have flowed from a considerable amount of legislation. Another is that, as a result of their growing sophistication, the increased need to make decisions about their children's schooling, and increased rights to information about the school and their children's progress, parents have become much more involved in the education of their children. A third is the growing involvement of non-educational agencies, principally the social services, which has exposed the teacher to additional expectations.

Even this brief account of the extensive range of expectations attaching to the teacher is sufficient to indicate the need for the teacher to sustain a balance, a changing balance, between them. A balance of a kind might be predetermined by accountability procedures, and teachers must be ready to account *post factum* for this, but, in the large part, balancing competing, and sometimes conflicting, expectations must largely remain a matter for the exercise of teacher responsibility.

Clientele

Teachers have to make judgements between the competing interests of clients. Such judgements would not be necessary if all client interests were congruent, but this is not the case. Individual pupils, pupils as a group, parents, the community, the state, and society as a whole, have competing interests, except where a totalitarian state has attempted to define teachers' responsibilities in terms of meeting its exclusive

117

interests. Otherwise teachers must make competing judgements in a wide number of areas.

One of the distinctive characteristics of teaching as a profession is that its immediate clients, *pupils*, are for most of the time dealt with in groups. One of the essential components of good class management is to see that all pupils are given the same degree of attention. This is also true, to some degree, of most professionals, since, although they may deal with clients on an individual basis, there are resource limits to the time which can be devoted to any individual. However, time allocation in a classroom presents particular difficulties. It is an area in which accountability is problematic. Only by observing a teacher over a sustained period could an outsider determine whether that teacher's classroom management gave a fair crack of the whip – if that's not too unfortunate a term! – to each pupil. Since such sustained observation is not usually a possibility, and since it is very difficult to attribute the measured progress of each pupil in relation to the others to the classroom strategies of the teacher, this allocation must largely remain a matter for the individual teacher's professional reflection. It is, of course, an issue addressed in courses of initial teacher training. What initial teacher training courses have also addressed for many years is the problem of labelling. The deleterious effects of the negative labelling of pupils by sex, social class, ethnicity and a whole range of other characteristics and identities is well known, and the responsibility of teachers to avoid this practice is emphasized.

This even-handedness in relation to all members of a school class is difficult to achieve. But, in so far as it can be achieved, it is inimical to the interests of the *parents* of individual children as clients. One of the central problems of educational policy arises from the conflict between two principles: what parents want for the general good and what they want for their own children. This is a dilemma for the thoughtful parent. The paradigm illustration has for thirty years been the politician who has publicly espoused comprehensive education but has sent his or her own children to selective or even independent schools. Parents want teachers to be fair to all pupils but to spend more time with their own. Some parents would not even wish to pay lip-service to equity. Thus the teacher's commitment to equity, difficult though it may be to achieve in practice, is in conflict with the parent's understandable desire for preferential treatment. Since accountability in this area is difficult to achieve, there is no alternative to reliance on the exercise of responsibility and judgement by teachers.

The *community* as client is not easy to conceptualize. Given the degree of parental choice, the idea of a community as a geographical and social entity in relation to a school makes little sense. An approach which has somewhat more meaning is to limit the idea of a community to the parents of children in the school. Yet the constitution of governing bodies, determined in the way set out in the 1988 Education Act, is a method of increasing the accountability of a school and allows for community representatives other than parents. The government clearly hoped that these representatives would challenge what were seen as 'trendy' – to use a favourite term of obloquy – forms of progressivism by bringing perspectives from business and other non-education sectors. However, the appointment of such governors makes the concept of client somewhat unclear. Moreover, the development has had some unintended consequences. In some instances, powerful governors have pressed for special interests, (e.g. religious, ethnic) in the school curriculum, sometimes against the wishes of the majority of parents. In such instances, teachers, and particularly headteachers, have had to take a stand against these pressures based on their professional judgement about the needs of the majority of pupils and the interests of the majority of parents, thereby countering misconceived accountability measures with professional responsibility.

The *state* is clearly a very powerful client of the teaching profession. In a democracy the legitimacy of the state derives from the outcome of the election process and it is appropriate that it should have a powerful voice in determining the nature and quality of education because of its potential influence on the

119

economic, social and moral orders of society. As noted above, over a period of twenty years Britain has moved from a situation where governments had a somewhat *laissez-faire* approach to education to a highly interventionist stance with ever-increasing forms of accountability. In, the absence of a General Teaching Council – at least for England and Wales – and with the power of the teacher associations weakened through legislation, there are few conduits for alternative educational perspectives to those of the state. There is a case, and it is certainly one which is firmly held by the present government, that teacher professionality consists in delivering a prescribed curriculum in an efficient manner. This would, of course, represent a reconceptualization of the traditional idea of a profession. However, there are inherent limits to de-professionalization, or a reconceptualized professionalization as appropriate policies because of the endemic uncertainties of education. Moreover, it should be seen as a function of a profession to challenge government policies where these appear to be against the interests of pupils, parents, and society. This is particularly true where government does not seek, or chooses to ignore, the views of the profession, however widely held and however well argued, chooses to ignore also the advice of civil servants, and relies instead on the advice of small ideologically driven groups, or takes little external advice at all. This becomes particularly dangerous where ministers take personal positions on such issues as how best to teach reading or on what is to be considered the 'ending date' of modern history. A case where the teaching profession has taken a stand, so far without success, against a policy which is seen as contrary to the interests of parents is in the construction and publication of school league tables which have no value-added component. Here, responsibility has demanded a challenge to a misconceived mode of accountability.

The teaching profession is in no way 'above' the state. On the other hand, the state is not society, and governments can be elected which have a quite different approach to education than their predecessor. It is perhaps a function of the teaching professions always to act as a countervailing force, or, at least, to act as the flywheel of educational practice. 'Society' as client is perhaps too abstract a notion, but it is important to recognize that whoever, at any given time, represents the state cannot claim a monopoly of educational wisdom. Downey (1990) takes it as one of the criteria of a profession that it has a duty to speak out with authority on matters of social policy, going beyond the provision of a service to specific clients. He notes that teaching is in a somewhat different position from, say, medicine and law on this issue, but argues that it remains a responsibility of the teaching profession. He writes:

> Education is a subject-matter on which many people have, and reasonably have, a view. There always has been a public involvement in education and this has grown as part of the more general 'rights movements' of which consumerism is one form. The population as a whole is better informed and has more awareness of rights than formerly. As a consequence, the tendency is to require the professions to supply a service on demand, and according to the perceptions of the consumer rather than those of the professional. If this movement develops will it destroy the authority of the professions? Does it mean that teachers cannot speak with authority on education?
>
> In reply it might be said that this challenge to teachers does not undermine their authority unless they allow it to do so. What the challenge should do is to revitalise the profession because it threatens the complacency and conservatism which afflict any profession, and it compels teachers to communicate more effectively. True authority emerges when paternalistic authoritarianism is challenged. (p. 158)

The state is a powerful client for the professional services of teachers, and in recent years has increased central – and also local – modes of accountability which are congruent with national policy. There nevertheless remain inherent conflicts between the needs and expectations of different sets of clients which it is beyond the scope of accountability procedures to reconcile. The teaching profession will continue to play a key role in mediating these demands, and this requires the exercise of responsibility.

121

An example of a hitherto successful outcome of the accountability demands of government and the responsible reaction of the teaching profession has been in the area of teacher appraisal. Demands for the accountability of individual teachers inevitably led to proposals for teacher appraisal. Simplifying the history of this policy, one can say that successive ministers have seen appraisal as a means of bringing teachers 'up to the mark' and dismissing those who failed to achieve the appropriate standards. Successive ministers have also discovered that teacher competence and teacher effectiveness are not the simple concepts that they thought them to be. The teaching profession, represented by the teacher associations, all of whom accepted the principle of appraisal, through argument and through collaboration with LEAs in pilot schemes, succeeded in convincing the government that appraisal was best approached from the positive point of view of the professional development of the teacher rather than the negative point of view of managerial control (see Evans and Tomlinson, 1989).

Professionality

Responsibility can only be properly exercised where teachers are equipped with the necessary degree of professionality, and it is to this quality that we can now turn.

There are perhaps three levels of professionality. At the practical level, professionality entails a body of skill and knowledge which teachers must have if they are to be effective classroom practitioners. There may be broad agreement on the skills required for effective teaching at a general level – such as those embodied in the Council for the Accreditation of Teacher Education (CATE) criteria – but it is unlikely that there will be total consensus. Moreover, the equifinality of teaching ought to make one wary of over-prescription. The argument of Chapter 3 also warns against an over-simplistic approach to teachers' knowledge.

A second level of professionality lies in the capacity for exercising sound judgement. Despite a general agreement on the basic skills and knowledge which teachers need, there remain important areas in which teachers have to decide between a range of pedagogical options. Moreover, as indicated in the previous two sections, the competing expectations attaching to the teacher's role, arising from the fact that teachers have different sets of clientele, involve them in making judgements between competing demands.

A third level of professionality entails the efforts made by teachers to equip themselves with the competences required to make effective judgements. Three aspects of this third level have been selected for consideration. They are: professional development, reflectiveness, and ethics.

Over twenty years ago one of the present authors (Hoyle, 1974) drew a distinction between *restricted professionality* and *extended professionality* and listed some of the components of each. Briefly, restricted professionality was used to refer to a high level of skill in classroom practice and extended professionality to refer to a broader range of knowledge and skill which contextualized – and hopefully improved – classroom practice. This latter form of professionality is largely acquired through participation in a wide range of professional development activities, including attending in-service courses, reading the professional literature, visiting other institutions, collaborating with colleagues in such activities as formulating school policies and preparing action plans, undertaking small-scale research projects, etc. Over the past twenty years the professionality of most teachers has been extended. A culture of professional development has emerged in teaching, supported by increased levels of funding for in-service training (though changes in funding have recently been putting this development at risk), the growing emphasis on school-focused activities entailing greater professional collaboration, and the increasing importance of professional development as a factor in promotion.

The collaborative aspect of professional development is particularly important, However, although a capacity for making sound judgements is a vital quality for professionals to have, it is not one for which there are obvious forms of training. Individuals vary in their inherent capacity to make sound judgements and in the degree to which they can learn from experience. However, it is more likely than not that judgement is best learned in contexts in which one's decisions, or proposals, are open to the scrutiny of one's professional colleagues in the process of peer discussion. They will also, of course, be scrutinized in the process of *post factum* accountability.

It has to be said, however, that because of the endemic uncertainties in the educational enterprise there are inherent difficulties in evaluating the outcomes of decisions made, not least because of the equifinality factor. Nevertheless, learning can take place through a consideration of the unintended consequences of an action.

This brings us to the second component of professionality: reflection. This has long been recognized as an important element in the professional education of teachers. Courses of initial training have conventionally emphasized the importance of planning and *post hoc* reflection on lessons, often with written comments. However, in recent years, institutions of teacher education have recognized the importance not only of *post factum* reflection, usually linked with systematic and summative forms of evaluation, but also of reflection-in-action.

This approach has drawn support from the work of Chris Argyris and Donald Schon (Argyris and Schon, 1974; Schon, 1983, 1987), which has already been referred to in Chapter 3. These writers have been concerned to question the earlier received wisdom of inert bodies of knowledge being given life and meaning by being in some way 'applied' to client problems. Argyris and Schon (1974) distinguished between *espoused theory* and *theory-in-use* and explored the congruence, or otherwise, between them. More recently, Schon (1987) has emphasized the importance of *professional artistry*, i.e. 'the kinds of competence practitioners sometimes display in unique, uncertain, and conflicting situations of practice'. This concept raises the fundamental issues concerning the notions of professional knowledge which were discussed in Chapter 3. This artistry,

Schon believes, is made manifest through *knowing-in-action* and can be enhanced through *reflection-in-action*. The former is used

> to refer to the sorts of knowledge we reveal in our intelligent action – publicly observable physical performances, like riding a bicycle, and private operations like instant analysis of a balance sheet. In both cases, the knowing is *in* the action. We reveal it by our spontaneous skilful execution of the performance; we are characteristically unable to make it explicit. (p. 25)

The latter he describes as follows:

> Reflection-in-action has a critical function, questioning the occupational structure of knowing-in-action. We think critically about the thinking that got us into this fix or this opportunity; and we may, in the process, restructure strategies of action, understandings of phenomena, or ways of framing problems.
> (p. 28)

Reflection *on* action is the *post factum* assessment of one's professional activities which may take forms ranging from a more-or-less intuitive judgement of a mental replay of, say, a lesson, through to the objective, formal and summative evaluation. Reflection-in-action is different in that, as the term implies, the reflection is inherent in the professional process and not simply *post hoc*. Both kinds of reflection are integral to professionality.

Schon (1987) discusses ways in which reflectiveness, particularly reflection-in-action, can be developed in professional education. His examples come largely from the training of architects, but initial teacher training has widely adopted his approach, and it is a quality which needs to be encouraged and developed throughout a teaching career. It has to be said, however, that it is by no means clear how professional development can enhance this quality. There are two inherent difficulties. One is that teaching is largely a private activity and there are few opportunities for practitioners to observe other practitioners who are regarded as having, in Schon's terms, the 'wisdom', 'talent', 'intuition' or 'artistry' which are manifestations of reflection. Another is that – again as Schon points out, and as any teacher educator who has invited an outstanding practitioner to talk to his or her students knows – successful practitioners are not necessarily able to convey in words the essence of their art. Nevertheless, one can assume that in so far as this aspect of professionality can be transmitted, it is most likely to occur in the collaborative settings for professional development which are currently emerging.

The third element of professionality is that of professional ethics. There can be no disputing that responsible behaviour is ethical behaviour, but, of course, what is 'ethical' is a contentious issue. One can perhaps identify three main elements of a professional ethic for teachers.

One relates to behaviour towards clients and to the competence with which professional tasks are carried out. A central injunction is that a professional should not use his or her position to cause physical or mental harm to clients, to treat them as a means to obtaining various sorts of personal gratification, or to infringe their rights. They also embrace such requirements as punctuality, preparation, task completion (e.g. marking), the avoidance of unnecessary absence, etc.

A second covers behaviour which would undermine the position of colleagues as professionals by, for example, criticizing to clients the quality of their practice, intervening directly in their professional practice without due consultation, etc. This aspect of ethics is ultimately about pursuing clients' interests, but it also has a dimension of self-interest and can be used to protect professionals against legitimate criticism.

The third, and perhaps most important, aspect of ethics is an extension of the first. It is essentially concerned with according priority to client interests beyond the behavioural level indicated above. Whereas this covers behaviour that is governed by law, by a professional code, or by bureaucratic requirements, the third type can be governed by law or by a professional code only at a very general level. It refers to the ethics which govern differences in treatment. This is a topic of considerable current interest. Medical ethics is one of the major growth areas in applied philosophy and covers such issues as euthanasia, organ transplants and abortion. These are very contentious areas which can, sometimes be dealt with through legislation. But, even where legislation exists, some practitioners may place ethical considerations above legal considerations and risk prosecution for their stand.

That there is less current interest in professional ethics in education than in other areas of professional practice is, in part, understandable in terms of the immediate and, literally, vital consequences of professional decisions in other fields and the fact that the consequences of educational decisions are long-term, less dramatic and aggregative. Nevertheless, the neglect of ethical issues is a little surprising. The professional responsibilities of teachers discussed earlier in this chapter are underpinned by ethical values. For example, given that decisions about time allocation in the classroom have to be made, the competing values of elitism and egalitarianism have to be resolved. Professionality requires teachers to consider these issues. They can be addressed as part of the process of reflection on individual practice, or as part of the process of professional collaboration.

A broad distinction between accountability and responsibility has been drawn for the purpose of the present argument. Although using the term *accountability*, Eraut (1992) usefully lists a number of components of, on our usage, *responsibility*. These are:

- a moral commitment to serve the interests of clients;
- a professional obligation to self-monitor and to periodically review the effectiveness of one's practice;
- a professional obligation to expand one's repertoire, to reflect on one's experience and to develop one's expertise;
- an obligation that is professional as well as contractual to contribute to the quality of one's organisation;
- an obligation to reflect upon and contribute to discussions about the changing role of one's profession in wider society. (p. 9)

127

This is, admittedly, an idealized list, yet it is a useful reminder of the breadth of what is entailed in the initial training and further professional development of teachers. As such, it can act as a useful corrective to policies which would severely limit the depth and scope of teacher education.

Conclusion

This chapter has been concerned with the professional responsibility of teachers. A working definition distinguished between *accountability* and *responsibility*. The former was seen as a set of processes whereby professionals are formally accountable to their various sets of clients. Accountability can take the form of prior requirements defining the nature and scope of the teacher's work, or the teachers' *post factum* forms of accounting for their professional activities.

Responsibility was depicted as being broader than accountability. Responsible professionals take accountability seriously. However, because of the diffuse goals of education, the equifinality of pedagogy, the changes in policy which occur as a result of the changing political complexion of governments, the diverse expectations of teachers, the potential conflict between client needs, etc., accountability is not enough. Responsibility is the process whereby a teacher, or a collectivity of teachers, further ensures that the interests of clients are met. They must be pro-active and act as principals as well as agents. Thus, accountability can be seen as the convergent principle, responsibility the divergent principle. Teachers will develop different ways of meeting what they perceive their clients' needs to be. They will have different perceptions of their roles and different styles. Accountability will guard against too much divergence.

Responsibility clearly implies a degree of autonomy and requires from clients a degree of trust. This trust is guaranteed through the professionality of teachers, which embraces a continuous development of knowledge and skill, the cultivation of judgement, and acceptance of a client-centred ethic.

6 The implications for teacher formation

Introduction

The institutions of teacher formation are at the moment in double jeopardy: indirectly through the changes in the educational conditions for which they are preparing teachers, and directly through the requirements and directives of recent legislation. Such developments raise, in a new form, old and persistent questions related to the knowledge and skills required of teachers as professionals, the sites in which these are best acquired, and the role of a profession as a counterforce to state power.

During the last decade, issues of teacher preparation and teacher professionalization have become central concerns for policy-makers both within and outside the teaching profession. Such anxieties are not a peculiarly British phenomenon, as demands for reform have become evident on both sides of the Atlantic, in mainland Europe, in the Middle East and in the Antipodes. In Britain, however, the motivation for change is linked to a wider political assault on the curriculum, the structural basis of educational institutions, and the professional status of the teacher. Indeed, it is ironic that during the present century, when the established professions of medicine and law have gradually developed extensive and sophisticated methods of professional preparation, the education of teachers faces a legitimacy crisis: one which calls into question the very basis upon which professionalization has traditionally been founded (Urban, 1990).

It is therefore not too much of an exaggeration to say that

129

teacher education and training are at the centre of the orbit of discussions surrounding educational policy. In both the popular and quality press, questions have been raised about the goals of teacher education, the content of courses, the pedagogy of teacher educators and the quality of the new teachers who make their way into our nation's schools. Many of these concerns have been echoed and exemplified in the pamphlets and writings of the radical right, who have fundamentally called into question the very existence of formal teacher preparation. The emergence of alternative routes into teaching, in particular the articled and licensed teacher schemes, the recently created school-based consortia and the establishment of the Teacher Training Agency, have put colleges, schools and Departments of Education on the defensive.

The contemporary scene

For those involved in teacher education, many of the above initiatives have been viewed as a further attempt to delimit and de-professionalize teaching while simultaneously being a threat to their very existence. Alternatively, supporters of such moves see the changes as part of a deregulation process whereby the monopoly of control of teacher formation is to be broken by ensuring that a variety of methods of entry coexist alongside the traditional university/college-based training. In this social market conception, traditional teacher education is depicted as being the most pernicious part of the educational establishment, injecting its pedagogical poison into thousands of new recruits. In reality, however, the contexts, control, content and personnel of formal teacher preparation are severely fragmented and diverse.

It is clear that, in terms of the range of courses being offered, the variety of institutions involved and the contrasting professional and academic communities that support it, formal teacher education in no way corresponds to the unified monopoly supplier or purveyor of doctrine that is depicted in popular demonology. None the less, successive Conservative governments of the 1980s and 1990s, with their combination of neo-liberal and statist ideology, have led the attack on the Teacher Education Departments which seem to represent the last vestiges of the post-war education consensus by continuing as bastions of liberal progressive pedagogy. This attack has rested on the linkage between the spectre of declining standards and the emergence of child-centred pedagogies; teacher educators have thus become the convenient scapegoats in the Conservatives' quest to restore British education to its pre-1960 position. To achieve this, their policy for teacher education hinges on three not always complementary strands.

The first is organizational, and concerns the need to control the diversity of courses and provision to ensure an adequate supply of high-quality teachers (a position likely to be taken by governments of every political persuasion). This has become even more important since the instigation of the Education Reform Act and the need to ensure a supply of teachers who are trained to teach the National Curriculum. For instance, if more mathematics, science and foreign languages are meant to be taught, then the government is now accountable for delivering teachers from higher education into the classroom. In the past this responsibility has been more diffuse, relying on an informal alliance of local authorities, schools and central government. Nowadays, however, the balance may be harder to strike, given the concentration of power at the centre and the lack of flexibility at a local level (Judge, 1989).

In addition, it is essential that new teachers be knowledgeable about the programmes of study and the assessment structure. The former, in particular, brings in new problems associated with subject knowledge which may require further controls, especially in undergraduate teacher education programmes, and may also eventually force the state to intervene in the mechanisms that control higher education. (Judge, 1989) Finally, ensuring that standards of training are of a similar quality in various parts of the country and that the courses replicate themselves over a period of time are likewise both vital if overall standards are to be consistent.

The second strand is ideological. Ideology is central to politics, and every political party seeks to impose its set of values after receiving a democratic mandate. The Conservative Party at successive elections has stood on a restorationist or back-to-basics platform in education: a policy that can be traced back to the Black Papers of the late 1960s.

The third strand is economic. The central message of Thatcherism was the unleashing of the forces of capital to regenerate a hapless corporate economy, a policy that was to have clear implications for institutions of teacher formation. As Hartley (1991) points out, for capitalism and democracy to survive and flourish, systems must try to fulfil two basic needs – accumulation and legitimization (O'Connor, 1973) – which were the basic tenets of Thatcherism. Education, claims Hartley (1991), is crucial to both: schools train and differentiate future employees, thereby helping accumulation; on the other hand, teachers can also inculcate a set of behaviours that will help them to adjust to life and work in a capitalist society, thereby legitimizing the former. In the 1980s, then, a competitive market-led structure was grafted on to the professional rhetoric of the previous decades and, in order to fulfil their role in this process, new teachers had to be rapidly socialized into the prevailing orthodoxies (Hartley, 1991). In this way, teacher education policy was cast within the net of economic liberalism and power was gradually taken out of the hands of the university and college professionals and placed under the more diffuse control of state quangos and school hierarchies. The process by which this was achieved is examined in the following section.

Teacher education reconstructed, 1973–93

Since the early 1970s there have been a number of policy changes related to teacher education, a pattern that led McNamara (1992) to comment that 'tinkering with the content of teacher education in the name of reform is becoming something of an end in itself' (p. 274). Despite current fears, very little time has been spent examining these changes and the ways in which particular discursive strategies and the political power underpinning them have been responsible for the shaping of policy. This section provides a detailed analysis of the reform rhetoric by treating the multiplicity of documentation surrounding initial teacher training as *founding texts* in which power and ideology manifest themselves. For the purpose of the investigation, the texts are categorized into three genres (Bhatia, 1993): the genre of the professional report (HMI Reports, etc.); the genre of the official report (DES circulars, speeches by politicians, CATE notes, etc.), and the genre of the polemical pamphlet (Centre for Policy Studies, The Social Affairs Unit, etc.). Following Swales (1990), a genre is defined as

> a recognizable communicative event characterized by a set of communicative purpose(s) identified and mutually understood by the members of the professional or academic community in which it regularly occurs. Most often it is highly structured and conventionalized with constraints on allowable contributions in terms of their intent, positioning, form and functional value. These constraints are often exploited by the expert members of the discourse community to achieve private intentions within the framework of socially recognized purpose(s). (p. 13)

In examining the conflicting and changing patterns of discourse within these three genres, this section will illustrate the ideological and political basis upon which current reforms in teacher education have been built, and aims to show how the discourse on teacher education has been appropriated, reshaped and eventually reconstructed by the state. In order to understand how a great many of these issues were addressed, we turn first to the changes in policy which have affected teacher education, looking particularly at the ways in which discursive shifts have been introduced into the policy agenda in order to generate change in initial teacher education.

Following Gottlieb (1992), the documents under review are treated as problematic and discursive events within which particular ideologies manifest themselves. The information

133

contained within the material is analysed not in terms of the validity of the claims in relation to truth or falsehood, but, rather, it is judged on its ability to persuade and to shift the professional agenda and thereby to alter both the substance and structure of policy and practice.

A central concept in the analysis is what Ranson (1993) has termed the 'commodification of discourse'. This is the process whereby institutions whose concern is not primarily that of producing commodities in the narrow economic sense come to be organized and conceptualized in terms of production, distribution and consumption. In initial teacher education the commodified educational discourse has become dominated by the technological and specialist vocabulary of business and the market-place. Professional learning has therefore been reworded and made dependent upon the language of behaviourism, a process which has manifested itself in the prominence of outcomes, in particular the stress on skill transfer, skill training and competency.

A further element in this process has been the use of metaphoric language. Metaphor has traditionally been thought of as a function of literary language; a way of embellishing text to improve understanding and readability. However, far from being a linguistic decoration, Taylor (1984a) claims that metaphor can be viewed as a 'ubiquitous feature of our thinking and discourse, the basis of our conceptual systems by means of which we understand and act within our worlds' (p. 5). Lakoff and Johnson (1980) have further claimed that metaphors are pervasive in all sorts of genres and are central to the way in which we think and act. Gottlieb (1992) similarly feels that metaphor is part of the process of *recontextualization* whereby a term from one frame of reference is transferred to another with the aim of changing its meaning.

This section therefore highlights *recontextualization* as a central feature of the discourse by showing how familiar concepts within one context are reconstructed in new and often unfamiliar ones. In order for such *recontextualization* to take place, the creators of policy have to construct new meanings for basic

134

terms that are deeply embedded within the old tradition. Gradually, over time, these terms take on new meaning and become translated into the new lexicon, thus completing the process of reconstruction. Given that these changes are longitudinal, we begin our analysis in the 1970s and trace the changes through to the present day.

During the early years of the decade, the declining birth-rate, the reorganization of secondary schools and the emergence of new conceptions of both curriculum and pedagogy brought teacher education close to the top of the educational agenda. Teacher preparation, it was felt, needed a long-term vision combined with structural changes that would bring order to a diverse and diffuse system. Such issues had been addressed by Robbins a decade earlier, and, despite the increasing popularity of the B.Ed., there was still little overarching conception of the role of teacher education.

The James Report of 1972 brought together a considerable body of evidence about teacher education. The Report and the Select Committee that preceded it were set up in response to a mixture of demographic, economic and professional concerns. Up to the early 1970s, as Taylor (1984b) has shown, initial teacher education had undergone a process of development which was characterized by relative cross-party agreement. In the main, teacher preparation was viewed neutrally, and the only contentious issues tended to be those associated with supply and recruitment. It was generally accepted that the purpose of teacher education was to produce high-quality teachers rather than to sustain any notions of ideological purity (Taylor, 1984b).

Despite recommending an elongated process of professional development and the linking of initial teacher training with the processes of professional development, the Report did little to create standardization. At the core of the proposals was the desire to maintain and develop the status and autonomy of the profession in a time of educational change by offering a diet of extended professional learning spanning the first five years of service. Above all, the Report continued to respect the right

135

of the profession, and the Institutions of Higher Education, to control and deliver courses of training within nationally set guidelines for recruitment, and the profusion of professional terminology in the Report reflects the continued consensus and support for the policy of organizational professionalism.

Many of the practical recommendations of the Report, however, floundered in the deteriorating demographic and economic conditions which continued to plague the decade. By the late 1970s the numbers in training had contracted, as had the resources being put into education as a whole. Various research studies also revealed the continued unevenness of provision and highlighted the continuation of a mix of the apprenticeship, academic and applied traditions. By the end of the decade, issues surrounding teacher formation had swung away from those concerned with structure and organization to more fundamental concerns associated with content and process (Alexander, 1984). This coincided with a general shift towards accountability in educational policy, in line with Callaghan's Ruskin College Speech and with developing internal criticisms about the apparent failure of the rational approach to teacher education to bring about desired improvements in teachers' expertise (UCET, 1979). This conglomeration of concerns found a convenient home in the Thatcherite critique of the political economy, homing in, as it did, on apparently falling standards and the need to tame an over-ambitious and powerful educational establishment.

Despite the unashamedly ideological slant of Thatcherism, the early years of the 1980s showed no real signs of the cataclysmic shifts in policy that were to usher in the 1990s. The three main HMI Reports of 1981, 1982b and 1983b all supported and reflected the professional lexicon which had been established in 1944 and reinforced in the James Report. The first Report (HMI, 1981) is sprinkled with the language of partnership and co-operation and goes out of its way to stress the interdependence of both schools and Higher Education Institutions in the quest to produce 'thoughtful, skilful teachers' who could respond to the 'complex demands of schools' (p. 6). In addition, the Report suggests that the pedagogy of teacher education (another unstudied problem) move away from the didacticism of the lecture format to the use of more user-friendly approaches, including seminars and workshops as forums for discussing and commenting on the students' own experiences. Central to this, claimed the Inspectorate, should be the process of self-evaluation, and the Report encouraged teacher educators to address the students' *'culture of observation'* (Lortie, 1975), which they claim was a continuing barrier to the development and effective deployment of new teaching strategies.

However, by 1983 the government's need for greater clari-fication of the processes involved in teacher education, com-bined with the continuing autonomy and diversity of courses, began to influence even the traditionally independent HMI. The Report of that year, entitled *Teaching in Schools: The Content of Initial Training*, reflected many of the concerns of the profes-sion (particularly as they had been articulated in the 1979 Universities Council for the Education of Teachers (UCET) Report) as well as the concerns of the government. The tone of the document is more prescriptive, and indicates that the profes-sional lexicon, so much in evidence in previous decades, was coming under review. The sentences are declamatory, and the falling cadences suggest a less advisory and more inspectorial tone, claims Fish (1987), while the phraseology is also indicative of a more narrowly defined, skill-centred occupa-tional lexicon, which was to gain in currency as the decade evolved.

Thus the UCET paper had become the starting-point for change in initial teacher training, and both HMI and govern-ment were to place many of its pronouncements within their discourse, thereby subtly incorporating the language of the pro-fession into their own ideological remit in order to persuade and control those who organized and delivered teacher education courses. Within three months of the HMI Report a White Paper on Teaching Quality appeared, and within eighteen months the Secretary of State had issued Circular 3/84 (DES, 1984), which set out a framework for the establishment of the Council for the

Accreditation of Teacher Education (CATE) and the rules by which courses of initial teacher training could gain accreditation.

The early commodification and technologization of language found in the 1983a HMI Report was further extended in the Circular. This document gave political and organizational direction to many of the semantic shifts alluded to above. The process of recontextualization was central; here, statements relating to the content and structure of courses appear not always to contradict the professional register found in earlier documents. Instead, the designations on admission, selection and the compartmentalization of time for various aspects of courses sustain a network of meaning between the old lexicon and the new. Such continuity can be explained by the state's lack of an appropriate and new language for presenting their ideas and also by the strategic need to keep the support of the professional community.

In the following extract we see teacher education institutions being directed to establish partnerships with schools, and the text stresses the importance of allowing serving teachers to play an influential role:

> Institutions in co-operation with LEAs and their advisers should establish links with a variety of schools and courses should be developed and run in close working partnership with those schools. Experienced teachers from school – sharing responsibility with the training institutions for the planning, supervision and support of students' school experience and teaching practice – should be given an influential role in the assessment of student teachers' practical performance.
>
> (HMI, 1983b, p. 4)

Such exhortations were followed by demands that tutors involved in training should have recent and relevant school experience and that primary courses in particular spend a minimum number of hours (100) on language and mathematics. The latter pre-dates the government's later obsession with teaching students to deliver the National Curriculum and the associated need for extended subject knowledge.

138

Despite the shifts, the Circular still kept itself within the bounds of professional acceptability and stressed the need for courses to show evidence of 'greater collaboration between colleagues' and for students to be encouraged to 'reflect on and learn from their classroom experiences' (p. 26). Nevertheless, much of the language used gives the impression of continuity while, at the same time, presenting new semantic networks associated with the practicality ethic. For instance, it states that 'educational and professional studies should provide students with an adequate mastery of the basic professional skills' (p. 28). In this sense, the discourse of the teacher education curriculum can be seen as going through a process of translation from one paradigm to another (Gottlieb, 1989). Underpinning this embryonic discourse of occupational control was the establishment of CATE; a move which, according to Barton *et al.* (1992), represented a further tightening of the grip of the state on the institutions of teacher education.

Although the workings of CATE were not to interfere with the traditional autonomy of higher education, all courses had to be vetted by local and national committees and then referred to the Secretary of State for final clearance. The appointees to CATE, however, were all within the personal patronage of the Secretary of State (CATE Note 1), while the local committees were to act as filters for the national committee (CATE Note 2) as well as giving detailed guidance on course structures in terms of subjects and their application (CATE Note 3). The latter, in fact, was a direct response to the criticism that too many courses, particularly undergraduate ones, were intellectually undemanding (CATE Note 4), and stressed the need for schools and higher education institutions to enter into more positive partnerships.

CATE was therefore to be the government's watchdog; the institution which would oversee course provision, ensure higher standards and control the diversity which was still a major feature of the training scene. Furthermore, the organization set in motion a revision of courses within schools of education and colleges. By the late 1980s the changing atmosphere outside

139

universities and colleges was also having an effect. The Education Reform Act of 1988 aimed at revolutionizing the school
and curriculum structure, and at the centre of the policy were
the twin objectives of driving up standards while at the same
time reducing public expenditure. Essential to this conception
of policy was the need to roll back the state and to base reforms
on the exigencies of the market-place. To ensure success,
however, the government had to take control of policy at the
centre.

In teacher education, this policy first manifested itself in Circular 24/89 (DES, 1989b) and in the documentation surrounding the introduction of the Licensed Teacher Scheme. Both
documents are replete with the commodified and technicist
language of the time, and the central ideological thrust grew out
of the increasing right-wing attacks on teacher education
establishments and the caricaturing of the role of theory in
training courses (McIntyre, 1992). These documents virtually
completed the translation of language from the professional to
the occupational lexicon. This can be seen in the increased use
of market-orientated metaphors which were beginning to
impregnate not only the language of education but also the
public services at large. This gradual commodification of
educational language saw children recast as Age Weighted
Pupil Units or clients, parents as customers, teachers as
deliverers and schools as businesses or units of production.
This language of entrepreneurial capitalism, as Hartley (1991)
points out, was part of a deliberate drive to change the mindsets
of those in public service while, at the same time, introducing
the psychology of the market mechanism to control public
finances.

Of central importance was the heavy emphasis placed on the
scrutiny and monitoring of courses. In outlining the reshaped
CATE frame of reference, Circular 24/89 (DES, 1989b) said
its role would be to 'monitor approved courses to ensure they
meet the criteria' and 'to keep the criteria for course approval
under review', and local committees were to have an increased
role in the 'scrutiny and monitoring of courses'. Such language,

as Wilkin (1990) points out, is hardly the type associated with professionals.

The introduction of the National Curriculum also played a crucial role in this translation of language. Student teachers were now required to have 'skills in the evaluation and recording of pupil performances including, in particular, the testing and assessment requirements related to the National Curriculum and, where relevant, the preparation of groups for public examination' (DES, 1989b, p. 406). The document also reveals the government's growing concern in education with the management of pupils' behaviour, presaging much of the recent advice on discipline and control (Wilkin, 1990). The paper continues its exhortations by demanding that courses 'contain compulsory units and clearly identifiable elements of practical teaching which will develop in students skills in the effective management of pupil behaviour' (DES, 1989b, p. 406). The Circular is also important in its attempt to establish the role of the teacher in the training process, and on page 409 alone the term 'serving teacher' is used no less than fourteen times.

The Qualified Teacher Status document, on the other hand, uses an impersonal language form reminiscent of legal documents and administrative concerns. (Wilkin, 1990) In effect, it is the language of deregulation, and places the Licensed Teacher Scheme within a privatization framework. The changes, claims the document, will create a 'simpler, more effective system of gaining Qualified Teacher Status' by opening up 'non-standard routes'. The document also makes a clear link between the emergence of delegated budgets and the desirability of schools taking responsibility for recruitment and training according to a business model. The problem of 'cost effective recruitment' is high on the agenda, and schools are encouraged to create their own training structures within a loose national framework, and the document stresses that the best people to make judgements about quality in teaching are the Local Education Authority, professional staff, and those 'charged with the management of schools'. This document was later followed by the National Curriculum Council guidelines for the training of licensed, articled and student teachers, which established emphatically the competences upon which courses should be based.

Central to these changes is the technologization of language, best represented in the competency movement touched on above. It is clear that the emergence of this discourse was not accidental, but formed a crucial part of the wider managerial approach to education exemplified in the accountability movement outlined in Chapter 4, a process which has been operationalized in the moves to establish teacher appraisal and performance-related pay (Short, 1985; McNamara, 1992). McNamara (1992) has carefully traced the origins of the use of the language of competency and claims it is part of a coherent policy on the part of the policy-makers to change both the form and substance of traditional teacher formation.

Although traces of the term can be found in early documents, such as the James Report, it only gained currency in the late 1980s, alongside the emergence of the National Curriculum. Indeed, much of the language is derived from the Curriculum's obsession with targets, levels and quantifiable outcomes. For example, in 1988 HMI felt that 'more attention should be given to defining levels of competence in different professional skills' but shied away from a closer delineation because of the complexities and the failure of earlier attempts. In Circular 19/89 a framework for competences is offered and is linked to the emergence of the Licensed Teacher scheme, while the Report, consisting of 'Other Trainers' Views' of teacher education, stressed the need for outcomes to be tabled because, at present, course design appeared to be

> back to front. Instead of starting with an explicit definition of the knowledge, understanding and skills needed by a teacher and then devising suitable courses, teacher trainers built their courses around certain components which had to be included to meet the Secretary of State's criteria. They were explicit concerning inputs and generally let outcomes remain implicit.
>
> (p. 4)

Prior to the competency movement, teacher educators had

traditionally claimed their authority, autonomy and control over the training of teachers by supporting a conception of professionalism which stressed the non-routine, value-laden, complex and interactive nature of teachers' work. Thus, they could point to the specialist expertise and judgement needed to teach effectively, and stressed the importance of their role as gatekeepers to the profession. The state, however, was busy redrawing this definition of professionalism by continually referring to outputs, in terms of both the National Curriculum and teacher performance, thereby introducing a conception of teaching based on delivery and didacticism. Thus the state, in linking various occupational services to the principles of technicality, was aiming to destroy the ideological and practical basis of indeterminacy and, at the same time, laying the foundations for a new conception of teaching.

The orders for the National Curriculum and the process of reform in teacher education are linked in this context. In the National Curriculum Council document on the training of student, articled and licensed teachers, the phraseology is strewn with references to delivery; in fact, of the seven areas of knowledge and skill outlined as necessary for new teachers, six are prefixed with a verb associated with delivery. These areas are framed mostly in behaviourist language, and this further exemplifies the correlation between the metaphor of delivery and the construction of teacher education around measurable, definable and observable outcomes. These add up to what Jessop *et al.* (1988) have termed the 'Conservative productivist ideology'.

Circular 9/92 (DFE, 1992), which was issued in the months following Kenneth Clarke's North of England Conference Speech in January 1992, laid down definitively the competences that would in future underpin the outcomes of teacher preparation. Again, the language mirrors the government's fascination with production and control. In terms of subject application, newly qualified teachers would have to demonstrate their competency in their ability to produce lesson plans, employ teaching strategies and present subject content, and demonstrate an ability to select and use resources.

Another feature of this recontextualization process can be found in the over-wording of documents. This has been seen as an 'intense preoccupation, pointing to "peculiarities" in the ideology of the group responsible for it' (Fowler, 1988, p. 24). This over-wording is often linked to an obsession within the texts with the ideological projection of a particular form of teaching. This can manifest itself in an over-emphasis on the weaknesses of a projected target and the stress on the need to correct the deficiency by regular doses of technical training (Fairclough, 1992). The recent Blue Paper outlining the government's intention to set up the Teacher Training Agency illustrates this most markedly. Early on in the document (para. 3) teachers are perceived as deficient, so much so that the government aims to 'ensure that teachers are better fitted to play a central role in implementing the new policies and achieving higher standards'. The use of the occupational delivery terminology is central, and in the following paragraph the Blue Paper outlines the principles upon which the reforms in teacher education will be based.

The general principles which underpin the reforms in teacher education already in hand and further developed in this paper are common to all occupations. They include:

a concern to raise educational standards and levels of skill, and to equip people to cope with change;

a growing emphasis on the competences necessary for effective practice;

the importance of training being closely linked to its practical application;

the need for continuing training and development through working life;

increasing the effectiveness of expenditure on training.

The use of the terms *training* and *effectiveness* linked to the apparent need to raise the professional skill of teachers implies a deficit view of current practices and an obsession with wider economic and political concerns. In addition, the language illustrates the urgency by which the government seeks to extend its ideological and political control over teacher education in order to force a technological reconceptualization of the process of teaching and learning based on the 'simplisms of productivity and accountability' (Diamond, 1991, p. 1).

Another crucial aspect of the reconstruction of teacher education over the past two decades has been the way in which the state has hijacked the language of democracy in order to justify its position and recontextualize discourse, thus making the presentation of its reforms more acceptable to the sceptical reader. In teacher education this has meant couching those reforms in the language of professionalism and partnership while, at the same time, deliberately working towards the redefinition and readjustment of each.

In teacher education this has been achieved through creative word-meaning. Raymond Williams cogently pointed out the importance of clusters of words and meanings to create new and various interpretations. 'Partnership' is such a term. Its use has been central to all the discussions surrounding the development of teacher education since McNair in 1944. As a term, its very elasticity of definition has allowed the state and the profession to create new meanings around it, a process which reflects the desire to claim the moral high ground in teacher formation.

Word meanings clearly do not always accord with accepted dictionary definitions, and often those in political control have a creative attitude to meaning and treat terms as exploitable and changeable resources. This creative use of language is characterized, according to Fairclough (1992), by ambiguities and ambivalences. The term 'partnership' illustrates how the meaning potential of a key word can be ideologically and politically invested during the discursive construction of policy within teacher education. Initially, the term has a variety of etymological aspects:

1. It is a process which has to be engaged in by various elements and at various levels of interest.

2. It has a quality reference in that it respects the dispositions of each of the elements and implies that either individuals or

institutions are ready to bury differences for the greater good.

3. It is contractual in that the agreed positions arrived at by mutual negotiation need some formal or informal binding.

However, the very ambiguity of the concept has allowed the state to exploit its value and create a situation whereby its own ideological preferences have been superimposed, thus creating a new set of meanings in which a particularly narrow conception of partnership has become paramount. The various official and unofficial documents emanating from government show how different texts highlight different senses of the term, not necessarily by promoting one to the exclusion of others, but by establishing a particular configuration of meaning that fits the ideological and political demands of the time.

During the 1950s and 1960s, for instance, partnership was seen as a desirable state, an ideal which could bring together both sides of higher education into harmony and thereby improve the professional development of novice and more experienced teachers. In this sense it was not an end in itself, but more a means of establishing greater credibility and status for courses and teachers alike. Thus the pronouncements were suggestive and rhetorical rather than prescriptive, and the term therefore became invested with a professional meaning that was broadly recognizable despite being unevenly applied.

Partnership for those professionally involved in teacher education was the watchword of the 1980s. The government's exhortations and demands were often confirmatory of a trend that had begun in the 1970s with some exemplary models of partnership. Dismay at the failure of the rationalist tradition to bring about improvements in training, and the rise of reflective practice as a major innovation in the 1980s, saw closer links with schools as providing the answer to the often apparently insoluble problem of the theory–practice divide. So, just as the government was redefining the concept, those involved in formal teacher education were busy revising courses so that their own rather different notion of partnership could be realized.

Wilkin (1990) has illustrated this by comparing a CNAA (Council for National Academic Awards) document and Circular

3/84 (DES, 1984). She shows very clearly how two opposing conceptions of partnership emerged during the early 1980s: the first, which was favoured by the government, was an 'equivalent relationship' which characterized tutors and teachers as being virtually the same, there being no significant differences in terms of expertise or role – a conception contradicted by both the UCET document of 1979 and the various HMI Reports of the period. The second, 'complementary role', was the subject of the CNAA documentation and emphasized reciprocal interdependence and celebrated the importance of tutors' and teachers' different roles yet collaborative relationship. Thus, as Wilkin (1990) claims, the Circular presaged further government policy in terms of school-based training by blurring the distinction between teachers and tutors, by rarefying the role of theory and by caricaturing professional knowledge of teacher educators as impractical.

The second complementary conception was also supported by numerous HMI Reports. In 1988 a Report outlined the Inspectorate's version of partnership, seeing it as being most successful when 'the contributions of teacher and tutor were complementary' (p. 143) and, furthermore, stating that partnership was a state in which 'teachers and tutors are equal'. The Inspectors go on to give numerous examples of good relationships between teachers and tutors and illustrate how, in unison, they can enhance students' work. In 1991, in a Report entitled *School-Based Initial Training in England and Wales* (HMI, 1991b), HMI further emphasized this complementary relationship by stressing that 'The present system of initial teacher training in England and Wales is based upon a partnership between higher education and schools. Their contributions are complementary and both are necessary' (p. 3).

In the same document, HMI went on to attack the shortcomings of the apprenticeship approach to teacher formation and emphasized that good courses were characterized by overlap and interdependence and that the concept of school-based training rests on more than just time spent in schools. HMI then continued to speak the language of professionalism and reiterated throughout its document the high-quality and cost-effective training that the present system delivered.

By 1989, however, the government was determined that an occupational conception partnership should be developed, and Circular 24/89 (DES, 1989b) limits the responsibilities of the tutor to those of vague role modelling, administration and the completion of recent and relevant school experience. Both roles are again undifferentiated, and the document goes further and carefully disengages theory from practice by relegating the vital topic of 'child development', for instance, to the educational or professional studies arena rather than keeping it within the remit of subject studies.

In the North of England Conference Speech in January 1992, the then Secretary of State, Kenneth Clarke, further clarified the new meaning of partnership. It was to be one in which teachers would be in the lead, and 80 per cent of courses would be school-based. Universities were to be reduced to a service capacity, providing input wherever the teachers decided. Theory was further rarefied, thereby permanently distinguishing it from the real world of practice. Thus the meaning potential of partnership was being reconstructed in terms of a hegemonic model of control. In this way, the New Right and the state manipulated the concept within the professional community so that teacher education was recast within the mould of its own ideological preferences and, to a certain extent, teacher educators were put into a position where they were seen to have colluded with their own marginalization. This final point was clearly put when Clarke boldly claimed that

> The gist of my proposals is very straightforward and, I would have thought, uncontentious in principle to most teachers who seem to welcome the idea of teacher training being more school- and classroom-based. Indeed, I know that many teacher trainers agree with me. The principle of making the training for a profession closer to where that profession is exercised ought not to be seriously challenged. It is indeed the basis upon which we train most other professions in this country.   (para. 43)

Another aspect of this creative wording has been the way in which partnership has become infected by the atmosphere of the social market. The contracts between schools and higher education are open to tender, with the price per student being decided by local market forces. Schools are encouraged to barter with higher education to gain the best deal, and to use their business acumen to negotiate positive terms. In Circular 14/93, *The Initial Training of Primary Teachers* (DFE, 1993b), the Department for Education claimed that transfer of funding from higher education institutions should be 'negotiated locally' (p. 12) and that the figures that emerge will act as a base level for the going rate for schools to opt into a partnership arrangement.

In the recent Blue Paper outlining the government's intended reforms for initial training the emphasis is also on economy and efficiency, the twin pillars of Conservative economic rhetoric. This is tied to an occupational substructure in which the responsibility of the Teacher Training Agency will be to 'promote the most cost-effective, high-quality initial training for the teaching profession. It will be expected to favour schools or institutions whose students are best fitted for their future employment' (p. 2). In other words, the Agency will help set up and monitor a social market in teacher education, and it is more than mere coincidence that Lord Skidelsky, Chairman of the Social Market Foundation, should introduce the Bill establishing the Agency in the House of Lords.

Thus the detailed course by course scrutiny of CATE is to be replaced by a consideration of quality at departmental and institutional level, with one of the major factors being the possession by student teachers of the necessary competences. Accountability in this new system will be assured by a combination of the rigours of the market-place and the close scrutiny of courses by the Agency and the Secretary of State – again, reflecting the ironic mix of central control and deregulation.

Higher education institutions are therefore being asked to reassess their roles as partners, a process which will now be guided by the ability of universities and colleges to reinforce and develop the subject knowledge necessary for teaching the National Curriculum programmes of study. In fact, the proposals are an extension of the arguments used by Clarke in his North of England Speech and exemplified in Circular 9/92 (DFE, 1992).

This new meaning of partnership is also closely associated with the continued attack on the theoretical nature of conventional teacher education. This attack sees higher education courses as over-theoretical and time-wasting, whose student teachers are forced to indulge the preoccupations of ivory-towered academics who propagate pernicious theory which is both harmful and irrelevant. The contradiction at the heart of this critique is that if such theory is indeed irrelevant and lofty, can it, at the same time, be harmful? Ironically the attack, in part, testifies to the effectiveness of traditional teacher preparation.

Nevertheless, in Clarke's speech the emphasis is placed on the importance of the role of 'serving teachers' in the training process, 'so that student teachers spend less time in teacher training colleges' (Clarke, 1992, para. 19) and more time at the chalk-face. He also went out of his way to further the view that the government's reforms had freed teachers from 'the dogmas about teaching methods and classroom organization' (para. 21). Training, he claimed, would henceforth be school-based and placed firmly in the hands of teachers, who will 'take the lead in terms of design and delivery of courses' and who will 'take major responsibility for the assessment of performance' (para. 22). In every respect, a rather unbalanced view of partnership. These obsessions – practical training, subject knowledge and classroom control – form the staple of the welter of prescriptions that have flowed from the Department for Education (DFE) in the ensuing twenty-four months since his speech.

A further characteristic of the reconstruction of teacher education has been the way in which the radical right wing of the Conservative Party has managed to take the ideological initiative and develop a critique of formal teacher education within the tradition of pamphleteering. For the purpose of this analysis we briefly explore the ways in which the language of one genre (the polemical pamphlet) is actively transmitted and transmuted into the language of another (the political speech), reflecting the increasing power of the ideological right and their associated pressure groups to influence and determine policy.

Early on, at the North of England Conference, the Secretary of State went out of his way to claim that his reforms would 'attract into teaching some of those who might have been put off by some of the orthodoxies of the past and by the fear of lacking the practical experience to cope in the classroom' (para. 12). This statement, despite having no basis in fact, is very similar to the sentiments expressed by Sheila Lawlor in her pamphlet *Teachers' Mistaught* (1990) when she claimed that 'in its present form, and despite the intentions of government reforms, training discourages good candidates from entering the profession and undermines the standards of those who do' (p. 3).

Official anxieties about the practicality of training were taken further by Clarke (1992) when he claimed that 'there is still some concern about whether new teachers are being adequately trained in the right way for success in the classroom' (para. 15), a point further exemplified in the Blue Paper, where it is claimed that a third of lessons taken by new entrants appeared to OFSTED (Office for Standards in Education) to be unsatisfactory. Such anxieties are reflected in the work of the Hillgate Group's 1988 pamphlet which attacked the lack of intellectual and practical experience of courses and recommended wholly school-based training. The accuracy of such statements is dispelled by HMI, who consistently demonstrate both a quantitative and qualitative improvement in teacher preparation programmes, both from students' own evaluations and in the opinion of headteachers. In 1988, for instance, their review of new teachers pointed out that over two-thirds of beginners were well-satisfied or reasonably well-satisfied with their training, and schools confirmed this by claiming that 95 per cent of new teachers were, at the very least, adequately prepared for their jobs. Such figures were an improvement on 1981 and are reflected in similar data from 1992.

151

Nevertheless, the deployment of the language of alarm, closely allied to the use of unsubstantiated evidence, is reminiscent of the method of the right-wing pamphleteers. And, when supported by the use of professionally orientated language, this has a twofold effect on the presentation of policy: first, it legitimizes the author's intentions, thereby helping the process of translation from one lexicon to another; second, it acts to distort and, at the same time, marginalize the case of those who favour school-based training from a professional perspective. This is further illustrated by Clarke's (1992) attempt to draw an analogous relationship between doctors, lawyers and teachers, aiming to show, somewhat seductively, that the established professions have always used 'supervised pupillage', with 'novices working alongside the best experienced members of the profession' (para. 22). Again, Clarke draws on Lawlor's (1990) ideas when she claims that a knowledge base in medicine and law is central to professional certification but that expertise in using the knowledge is only gained through practice and experience.

This view of the relationship between professional knowledge and professional practice in the traditional professions is discussed in Chapter 3. However, of greater importance is the fact that assertions are made without recourse to evidence of even the most rudimentary kind. Thus, various Secretaries of State have been able to caricature teacher education as an unfamiliar and rather remote world, full of vested interests and ideological prejudices.

Partnership: Panacea or palliative?

Since early 1992, course directors in initial teacher education establishments have been busy reorganizing and reformulating courses in line with the decrees outlined in Circular 9/92 (DFE, 1992). The document outlines the criteria for partnership and the basis upon which methods for ensuring new teacher competency should be built. These criteria have formed the foundation for the new generation of partnerships that have grown up since 1992.

Such moves have been complicated by disagreements inside the profession. David Hargreaves (1989), for instance, has proposed the dismantling and overhaul of the existing structure of teacher education. Combining the pluralist and professional discourse of the 1960s and 1970s with the technical and rationalist movement of the 1980s, he argues that giving teachers control and responsibility over professional training would not only enhance their professional status but also raise the quality of training and professional development. His belief in and advocacy of professional training schools along the lines of the teaching hospitals has forced teacher educators to defend their position on two fronts.

On a different tack, Harry Judge (1980) in his justification of the development of the Oxford Internship Scheme argued that practical attempts to professionalize teacher education conceal essential ambiguities. These relate, on the one hand, to the need to develop the status of teaching by continuing the role of university-based training while, on the other, ensuring that young aspirants have the competency that can only come through extended classroom experience. Judge went on to argue that the tensions would be eased if institutions of formal teacher preparation gave equal weight to both scholarly activity and professional service.

These two positions (Hargreaves, 1989; Judge, 1980) highlight the continuing tensions within the professional community itself about the future structure, management and delivery of initial teacher education. Within this context some institutions embarked on a radical rethink of partnership. At Oxford, Harry Judge announced the development of the internship scheme, with a curriculum and structure based firmly on research and scholarship on teacher education and on a close partnership with local schools. The negotiations and planning were long and detailed, and every step was supported by local authority funding. The final result was a course designed to overcome many of the intractable problems of traditional teacher education courses while, at the same time, being based firmly on a professional, collaborative conception of the processes involved in learning to teach.

Space does not permit a lengthy outline of the various aspects of the course (see Benton, 1990), but it has been lauded as the perfect model of partnership both by professionals and by those not usually drawn to praise. But how does the Oxford Internship Scheme fit within the wider context of the reconstruction of teacher education, and what separates the Oxford programme from the moves towards school-based training as advocated by the government and its right-wing ideologues?

An insight can be gained from the language and metaphors that underpin both models. In the occupational model the language is derived from behaviourism and the market. It is nakedly technicist and stresses the competency outcomes to be derived from practice as the main criteria by which fitness for entrance to the profession will be judged. The language of the Oxford partnership, on the other hand, is peppered with the vocabulary of the established professions: internship itself has connotations with early medical placements in hospital contexts; chartered intern status reflects the language of the actuary; clinical supervision represents an attempt to systematize the process of supervision; the emphasis on accessing 'professional craft knowledge' honours the practical knowledge of the practitioner; while the designations 'professional tutors' and 'mentors' are indicative of the ongoing attempt to raise the status of the school-based teacher educator.

The extent to which the Oxford model has influenced other courses, and the ways in which such courses have organized their partnerships, also needs to be examined. Detailed information is hard to come by, given the speed at which schools of education were forced to redesign courses along the lines outlined by Circular 9/92 (DFE, 1992). In fact, it seems that when partnership moves from the conception to reality numerous tensions and problems arise which throw the process of inter-institutional collaboration into sharp relief. Although the Oxford model is often desirable, the nuances of local school structures, the financial constraints and the burden of tradition have meant that many new arrangements have reflected more immediate concerns. Also, many schools of education were already moving in the direction of partnership before Circular 9/92 demanded it, but the short time-scale forced them into a whirlwind of change which Oxford did not have to suffer. In order to understand the workings of these new partnership arrangements at micro-level, two case studies of partnership are offered.

The Leicester scheme
At Leicester the government's insistence on the move to greater partnership and school-based training merely forced the pace of changes that were already evolving. Since the 1960s practising teachers had been closely involved in the training courses, a process pioneered by Brian Simon. Throughout the 1980s further links were established through the extension of IT-INSET activities, so much so that by the end of the decade there were a host of formal and informal collaborative activities. The existing partnership scheme demanded by Circular 9/92 therefore grew out of these developments.

Structurally, the course sees students spend two days a week for three weeks in clusters of partner schools during the early autumn term, followed by a six-week block of teaching practice in one of the cluster schools. They then spend eighteen days in schools during the spring term, followed by a second teaching practice block of eight weeks duration in different schools. Finally, they return to their partnership clusters for a further twelve-day block period at the end of the summer term.

The course is based around subject-specific method studies and more generic professional studies. Subject tutors therefore play a dual role by acting as both subject tutors and link professional course tutors. Student teachers are paired where possible in a subject department in school, and work closely with a designated co-tutor. Subject tutors liaise closely with these co-tutors to ensure integration of both content and process. In association with the co-tutors, schools also have designated professional tutors who liaise with the link tutors to ensure coherence and continuity.

The Secretary of State's decision to increase the amount of school-based training made very little difference to the Leicester scheme. However, concerns and problems have arisen in relation to the prescriptive nature of the government's concept of partnership, the pace of the reforms and the financial implications embedded within them. Beginning with the latter, it seems that the scheme already in place was based on the fact that university tutors would take most of the workload, a factor which correlated with the resources allocated to them. However, these economies of scale have been replaced by diseconomies of scale where perhaps five or more co-tutors are to be paid for doing the work previously done by one university tutor. This has clearly had an effect on the amount of resources which the School of Education can transfer to schools.

Many at Leicester also fear that the hurried nature of the changes will jeopardize the well-established harmonious working relationships and that schools are still relatively unprepared for the nature of the devolved responsibilities. So much so, that the danger is that without adequate resourcing and higher education support schools may struggle to manage their new training responsibilities and, instead, treat them as a low priority, bolt-on innovation (Kerr, 1994). In conjunction with this, many are concerned at the simplistic short-term and ideologically motivated changes which, when accompanied by financial austerity, leave very little room for manoeuvre. As a result, the revised criteria for partnership may undo all the local networks and the good practice that has been fostered through decades of self-critical hard work.

Lastly, the confrontational rhetoric and financial imperatives hidden within the documentation have given schools the impression that departments of education have large untapped resources which can immediately be transferred to them. This has led many headteachers to think more in terms of plundering the coffers than of any notion of a partnership based on sharing. The medium-term effects of the changes could lead to a number of scenarios: first, the university may consider opting out of initial teacher training if the cost becomes too great; and, second, if courses are to last beyond the period of transitional funding, then staff costs may have to be reduced if schools demand an ever-increasing slice of the cake. Inevitably the change in resources will mirror changes in roles and responsibilities. At Leicester the transfer of cash may well mean a gradual withdrawal of support from the university tutors, thus creating in the long-term the very division between theory and practice that so many staff have tried to eradicate.

The University of East Anglia
In 1991 discussions were set in motion to explore the nature of partnership in the light of the structural changes to schools' finances and management. This process was extended after the North of England Conference Speech in January 1992. Some headteachers expressed positive feelings towards the changes while others stressed a more cautious approach given the strain they were under to deliver the National Curriculum. The headteachers' working group rejected the Oxford model of internship on organizational grounds. Most urban secondary schools in the area are 11–16 and usually with a roll of under 600. To place students all year round in such small schools would not only result in a limited experience but, it was felt, would also prejudice the curriculum.

Circular 9/92 was therefore interpreted flexibly, with two school experiences taking place during the autumn and spring terms. The heads were also keen on the course being guided by action research principles (a factor closely related to the traditions of action research set up by John Elliot), but concern was raised about the relevance of an action research perspective within a competency based framework. Nevertheless, such principles guided the structure of the programme, which resulted in a complex mix of school-based and school-focused weeks in which students would be gradually introduced to teaching

157

through exploration and observation of their own and others' practice.

The problems which grew up alongside the development of the partnership mirror wider issues central to teacher education as a whole. In the first instance, very few teachers regard teacher education as problematic. Many therefore continue to operate on teaching practice conceptions of school experience. Second, many teachers, despite being involved at subject level in training for a number of years, professed very scant knowledge of the curriculum of the programmes. This was combined with a feeling of retrenchment by many teachers who were still labouring under the demands of the National Curriculum and assessment.

As a result, many concerns have arisen. First, there is very little understanding about what entitlement actually means in the context of teacher education. This leads on to a second concern, that of funding and resources relating to the demands of the role. Working closely with student teachers in a mentoring capacity is time-consuming and expensive, a factor closely associated to the issue of perception. If teachers and mentors see their role primarily as giving tips or recipes to student teachers within a survival framework, the training implications are immense and the support from higher education tutors is made even more important. However, the financial basis of the partnership means that tutors will increasingly be forced into a minimalist role as managers of schools of education and one-to-one tutoring will be seen as a luxury.

Conclusion: de-professionalization or professional regeneration?

Formal teacher preparation in England and Wales is now at a crossroads in its history. Opponents have argued (often in contradictory terms) that teacher education establishments peddle, at the same time, both dangerous and useless theory. Their answer has been the creation of a social market whereby schools compete openly with higher education institutions for the business of training.

We regret the primacy of this approach and its surrogate, the occupational model of teacher formation. To see initial teacher training as a process of rapid socialization into existing school frameworks based on a narrow apprenticeship approach and tested by reference to competency outcomes is dangerously perfunctory and ridiculously limiting. Becoming a teacher, as research has indicated, is cognitively, affectively and physically challenging. Student teachers enter training with a range of understandings and beliefs about their subjects, teaching, learning to teach and learning in general, based on their educational experiences up to that time. Helping them to address these issues is central to the concerns of teacher educators, who themselves have been largely drawn from the classroom and who have considerable teaching experience.

In terms of subject-matter knowledge, helping students to understand, reconceptualize and transform what they know so that children can learn is also a vital process. In conjunction with this, introducing them to the complexities of the National Curriculum at the four key stages and beyond requires considerable skill and care. Furthermore, supporting them as they come to terms with the inevitable emotional pressures and strains of being a teacher makes the job of the professional teacher educator wide-ranging, and nowhere in the official documentation are such abilities recognized.

On a wider front, the relationship between teacher education and the broader professional community is also central to the issues surrounding teacher preparation. However, the unitary notion of a professional community masks a vast array of competing positions which characterize a service profession such as teaching (Liston and Zeichner, 1990). In this sense, the role of teacher education is never static, but is constantly changing according to the particular educational traditions that predominate at any particular historical juncture. At present, the whole notion of a professional community, with its attendant issues of autonomy, responsibility and accountability, is under

159

pressure as the state seeks to redefine both the nature and substance of the curriculum, the organizational apparatus that supports it and the pedagogy that delivers it. The outcome of such deliberations will inevitably hinge on what happens to teacher education.

It is clear from the analysis presented in this chapter that the relative ease by which teacher education has been transformed is indicative not only of the power of the state but also of the relative weakness of institutions of teacher formation. Their standing within university culture, even during times of greater acceptance, was always fragile, and in many respects this lack of status reflects the position of teachers in the community at large. The relatively low standing afforded to teacher education has undermined continued attempts at developing the power and authority of teachers, a process that has not been helped by the amorphous mass that represents both the discipline and provision of education.

Recent changes to the curriculum and to the structure of schools have not helped either. New entrants are now being socialized into a professional community that is increasingly coming under the dictates of central government. What effects such pressures will have on the new generation of teachers is hard to gauge, but they are unlikely to view teaching in terms of an extension of their professional autonomy and judgement. Thus it is possible that the loss of university and college influence, combined with the increasing localization and utilitarian nature of in-service and pre-service training, may create a new generation of teachers who lack the spirit to fight for further professional status. Thus, the de-intellectualizing of teacher education and the devaluing of the credential attached to it may feed into the pool of new aspirants. This process will not only change the milieu of training and lower the status of both job and qualifications, but it could simultaneously narrow professional horizons so that improving delivery is the only desired outcome of professional training.

The changes in the 1980s to the curriculum, the structure of schooling and to teacher education have also meant that the

160

traditional independence of teacher education courses has gradually been eroded. The imminent formation of the Teacher Training Agency is likely to continue the process of de-professionalization which has been growing since the early 1980s. In reality, this could mean a substantial number of teacher education departments closing down or, at the very least, shedding their initial teacher training functions. And, even if many survive, it is possible that a number will be reduced to providing certification and to the delivery of basic services.

Alternatively, the present generation of partnerships may offer not only a lifeline but also the possibility of professional regeneration. Closer co-operation may eventually bring improvements in teaching and learning, since many of the new collaborative efforts have not been purely organizational but, in many instances, have been premised on the will to improve (Fullan and Hargreaves, 1992). As a result of partnership the profile of teacher education has risen in schools, and many teachers, as the case studies indicate, have been enhanced professionally by the greater contact and involvement with teacher educators. This process of collaboration, although in its infancy, may prove to be the basis upon which the future professional development of teachers can be built. In order for this to occur, teacher educators have to make it clear to both policy-makers and school personnel that the changes are beneficial and preferable to a wholly school-centred conception of teacher preparation.

For this to be achieved, the first priority must be to stay in the market. As pressure builds from school-based consortia, many vice-chancellors and college principals may feel that further investment in teacher education is not cost-effective. Survival is vital, and, as Erly and Greenberg (1992) have shown, partnerships in initial teacher education often begin in a mechanical fashion but, as they develop, trust and common agreement on the future emerges. A long-term vision is therefore central to a stable relationship.

Teacher education, then, urgently needs a unifying and clarifying agenda, and perhaps in the present political climate

161

it may be both politically astute and strategically sensible to follow the lead given by the Holmes Group in the USA. They advocate a form of teacher formation based on collaboration and the foundation of professional development schools linked to institutions of teacher education. The Group outlines six principles around which such partnerships should operate:

1. An emphasis on teaching and learning for understanding.
2. The development of a learning community.
3. An emphasis on enquiry and reflection.
4. An inclusivity that would make social barriers to education obsolete.
5. A commitment to life-long learning.
6. New organizational structures within and among professional development schools, universities and local communities.

In order for such proposals to form part of a coherent policy on teacher education, those involved must commit themselves to the current partnerships in the hope that when a political space eventually occurs the profession will be able to reassert democratic and professional control over the process of teacher formation.

Whatever the future holds, it is clear that politically orientated reforms are not the best foundations upon which to build secure long-term partnerships. As we have shown, the attitudinal, value-laden and locational tensions inherent in initial teacher training cannot be solved by recourse to a badly thought out legislative framework which merely seeks to arrange a divorce before the partners have really got to know each other. For, if this current generation of partnerships is to survive and move beyond the world of rhetoric and cliché, unilateral restructuring will not be sufficient, because what is needed is a long-term commitment which requires thought, vision and the creation of teacher education communities where

> purposeful preparation, mindful practice, critical reflection, mutual discourse and continuing inquiry are normal ways of working, not exceptional events ... [A]nd from the time student teachers begin seriously to hone their skills and to

assume their professional attitudes, the habits of reflecting, questioning and trying out and evaluating new ways of teaching – by themselves and with colleagues – should become embedded in their professional identity. (Holmes Group, 1986, p. 55)

Acknowledgement

We are indebted to both David Kerr (University of Leicester) and Chris Husbands (University of East Anglia) for their permission to use material from their case studies of the first year of partnership at their respective institutions. More detailed accounts can be found in John and Lucas (1994).

References

Alexander, R. (1984), 'Innovation and continuity in the initial teacher education curriculum', in Alexander, R. *et al.* (eds), *Change in Teacher Education: Context and Provision Since Robbins*, London, Holt, Rinehart & Winston.

Archer, M. (1982), *Social Origins of Educational Systems*, London, Sage.

Argyris, Chris and Schon, Donald (1974), *Theory in Practice: Increasing Professional Effectiveness*, San Francisco, Jossey-Bass.

Auld, R. (1976), *Report of the Public Inquiry into the William Tyndale Junior and Infant Schools*, London, ILEA.

Bacharach, Samuel B. and Lawler, Edward J. (1980), *Power and Politics in Organizations*, San Francisco, Jossey-Bass.

Bacharach, S.B. *et al.* (1990), 'The dimensionality of decision-participation in educational organizations: The value of a multi-domain approach', *Educational Administration Quarterly*, **26**, (2).

Ball, D.C. (1990), 'The mathematical understandings that prospective teachers bring to teacher education', *The Elementary School Journal*, **90**, (4), pp. 449–66.

Ball, S.J. (1992), 'The worst of three worlds: Policy, power relations and teachers' work', BEMAS research conference paper.

Ball, S.J. and Goodson, I.F. (1985), *Teachers Lives and Careers*, Sussex, Falmer Press.

Barber, M. (1992), *Education and the Teacher Unions*, London, Cassell.

Barton, L. *et al.* (1992), 'Experiencing CATE: The impact of accreditation upon initial training institutions in England', *Journal of Education for Teaching*, **18**, (1), pp. 41–59.

Becher, T. and Maclure, S. (eds) (1978), *Accountability in Education*, Windsor, NFER Publishing Co.

Bennett, N. and Carre, C. (1991), 'No substitutes for a base of knowledge', *Times Educational Supplement*, 8 November 1991.

Bennett, W.S. and Hokenstad, M.C. (1973), 'Full time people workers and conceptions of the "professional"', in Halmos, P. (ed.) *Professionalization and Social Change* (Sociological Review Monograph 20), Keele, University of Keele.

164

Benton, P. (ed.) (1990), *The Oxford Internship Scheme: Integration and Partnership in Initial Teacher Education*, London, Gulbenkian.

Bernstein, B. (1971), 'On the classification and framing of educational knowledge', in Young, M.F.D. (ed.), *Knowledge and Control: New Directions for the Sociology of Education*, London, Macmillan.

Bernstein, Basil (1975), *Class, Codes and Control, Vol. 3: Towards a Theory of Educational Transmissions*, London, Routledge.

Bhatia, V.K. (1993), *Analysing Genre: Language Use in Professional Settings*, London, Longman.

Broadfoot, P. and Osborn, M. (1988), 'What professional responsibility means to teachers: National contexts and classroom constants', *British Journal of Sociology of Education*, **9**, (3).

Broudy, H.S. *et al.* (1964), *Democracy and Excellence in American Secondary Education*, Chicago, Rand McNally.

Brown, S. and McIntyre, D. (1992), *Making Sense of Teaching*, Milton Keynes, Open University Press.

Butt, R.L. and Raymond, D. (1987), 'Arguments for using qualitative approaches in understanding teachers' thinking: The case of biography', *Journal of Curriculum Theorizing*, 7, (1), pp. 62–93.

Calderhead, J. (1989), 'Reflective teaching and teacher education', *Teaching and Teacher Education*, 5, (1), pp. 43–51.

Carr, W. and Kemmis, S. (1986), *Becoming Critical: Education, Knowledge and Action Research*, Sussex, Falmer Press.

Carter, K. (1990), 'Teachers' knowledge and learning to teach', in Houston, R. (ed.), *Handbook of Research on Teacher Education*, New York, Macmillan.

Council for the Accreditation of Teacher Education (CATE) (1985), *The Council's Approach to Accreditation* (CATE Note 1), London, HMSO.

CATE (1985), *Local Committees* (CATE Note 2), London, HMSO.

CATE (1985), *Subject Studies* (CATE Note 3), London, HMSO.

CATE (1986), *Links Between Initial Teacher Training Institutions and Schools* (CATE Note 4), London, HMSO.

CATE (1988), *The Selection of Students for Admission to Initial Teacher Training Course* (CATE Note 5), London, HMSO.

CATE (1992), *The Accreditation of Initial Teacher Training under Circulars 9/92 (DFE) and 35/92 (Welsh Office)*, London, HMSO.

CATE (1993), *The Initial Training of Primary School Teachers: Circulars 14/93 (England)*, London, HMSO.

Clark, C. and Yinger, R. (1988), 'Teacher Planning', in Calderhead, J. (ed.) *Exploring Teachers' Thinking*, London, Cassell.

Clarke, K. (1992), *Speech to the North of England Education Conference*, London, DES.

Connelly, M. and Clandinin, D.J. (1985), 'Personal practical knowledge and the modes of knowing: Relevance for teaching and learning', in Eisner, E. (ed.), *Learning and Teaching the Ways of Knowing*, Chicago, University of Chicago Press.

Connelly, M. and Clandinin, D.J. (1988), *Teachers as Curriculum Planners*, New York, Teachers' College Press.

Cunningham, P. (1992), 'Teachers' professional image of the press, 1950–1990', *History of Education*, **21**, (1), pp. 37–56.

Dale, R. (1981), 'Control, accountability and William Tyndale', in Dale, R. *et al.* (eds), *Education and the State*, Sussex, Falmer Press.

Darling-Hammond, L. (1989), 'Accountability for professional practice', *Teachers' College Record*, **91**, (1).

Davies, Celia (1983), 'Professionals in bureaucracies: The conflict thesis revisited', in Dingwall, R. and Lewis, P. (eds), *The Sociology of the Professions: Lawyers, Doctors and Others*, London, Macmillan.

Day, C. (1993), 'Reflection: A necessary but not sufficient condition for professional development', *Teaching and Teacher Education*, **19**, (1), pp. 83–95.

Denizen, N.K. (1991), 'Deconstructing the Biographical Method', paper presented at the American Educational Research Association Conference, Chicago.

Department of Education and Science (DES) (1972), *Teacher Education and Training* (The James Report), London, HMSO.

DES (1977a), *Education in Schools: A Consultative Document*, Cmnd. 6869, London, HMSO.

DES (1977b), *A New Partnership for our Schools* (Taylor Report), London, HMSO.

DES (1983), *Teaching Quality*, London, HMSO.

DES (1984), *Initial Teacher Training: The Approval of Courses*, (Circular 3/84), London, DES.

DES (1988), *Qualified Teacher Status: A Consultation Document*, London, DES.

DES (1989a), *Articled Teacher Pilot Scheme*, London, DES.

DES (1989b), *Initial Teaching Training: The Approval of Courses*, (Circular 24/89), London, DES.

Department for Education (DFE) (1992), *Circular 9/92*, London, DFE.

DFE (1993a), *The Government's Proposals for the Reform of Initial Teacher Training*, London, DFE.

DFE (1993b), *The Initial Training of Primary School Teachers*, (Circular 14/93), London, DFE.

Diamond, C.T. (1991), *Teacher Education as Transformation*, Milton Keynes, Open University Press.

Dingwall, R. (1976), 'Accomplishing profession', *Sociological Review*, **24**, (2).

Downey, R.S. (1990), 'Professions and professionalism', *Journal of Philosophy of Education*, **25**, (2), pp. 147–57.

Doyle, W. (1977), 'Learning the classroom environment: An ecological analysis', *Journal of Teacher Education*, **28**, pp. 51–5.

Doyle, W. (1983), 'Academic work', *Review of Educational Research*, **53**, pp. 159–99.

Doyle, W. (1990a), 'Classroom knowledge as foundation for teaching', *Teachers, College Record*, **91**, (3), pp. 347–59.

Doyle, W. (1990b), 'Themes in teacher education research', in Houston, R. (ed.), *Handbook of Research on Teacher Education*, New York, Macmillan.

Dworkin, G. (1988), *The Theory and Practice of Autonomy*, Cambridge, Cambridge University Press.

Edwards, A.D. (1992), 'Issues and challenges in initial teacher education', *Cambridge Journal of Education*, **22**, (1), pp. 283–93.

Elbaz, F. (1983), *Teacher Thinking: A Study of Practical Knowledge*, London, Croom Helm.

Elliot, J. (1990), 'Educational theory and the professional learning of teachers', *Cambridge Journal of Education*, **19**, (1), pp. 81–103.

Eraut, M. (1988), 'Knowledge creation and knowledge use in professional contexts', *Studies in Higher Education*, **10**, (2), pp. 117–32.

Eraut, Michael (1992), *Developing the Professions: Training, Quality and Accountability* (Professional Lecture), Brighton, University of Sussex.

Erly, M.C. and Greenberg, J.D. (1992), 'Inter-institutional collaboration: A descriptive model for improvement in teacher education', paper presented at an international seminar on teacher education, University of Groningen, Netherlands.

Etzioni, A. (1969), *The Semi-professions and their Organizations*, Glencoe, Free Press.

Evans, Alan and Tomlinson, J. (1989), *Teacher Appraisal: A Nationwide Approach*, London, Jessica Kingsley.

Fairclough, N. (1992), *Discourse and Social Change*, Cambridge, Polity Press.

Fenstermacher, G. (1986), 'Philosophy of research on teaching: Three aspects', in Whittrock, M.C. (ed.), *Handbook of Research on Teaching*, New York, Macmillan.

Fish, D. (1987), 'The initial training curriculum', in Golby, M. (ed.), *Perspectives on the National Curriculum*, Exeter, University of Exeter.

Flexner, Abraham (1915), 'Is social work a profession?', in *Proceedings of the National Conference of Charities and Corrections*, Chicago.

Fowler, A.F. (1988), 'Notes on critical linguistics', in Steele, R. and Threadgold, T. (eds), *Language Topics* No. 12, Amsterdam, Benjamins.

Freidson, E. (1970), *The Profession of Medicine*, New York, Dodd, Mead & Co.

Fullan, M. (1991), *The New Meaning of Educational Change*, London, Cassell.

Fullan, M. (1993), *Changing Forces: Probing the Depths of Educational Reform*, London, Falmer Press.

Fullan, M. and Hargreaves, A. (1992), *What's Worth Fighting for is your School: Working Together for Improvement*, Milton Keynes, Open University Press.

Gage, N.L. (1978), *The Scientific Base for the Art of Teaching*, New York, Teachers' College Press.

Good, T. (1992) 'Building the knowledge base of teaching', in Dill, D. (ed.), *What Teachers Need to Know: The Knowledge, Skills and Values Essential to Good Teaching*, San Francisco, Jossey-Bass.

Goodson, I.F. (1992), 'Studying teachers' lives: An emergent field of enquiry', in Goodson, I. (ed.), *Studying Teachers' Lives*, London, Routledge.

Gosden, P.H.J.H. (1972), *The Evolution of a Profession: A Study of the Contribution of Teachers' Associations to the Development of School Teaching as a Professional Occupation*, Oxford, Blackwell.

Gottlieb, E. (1989), 'The discursive construction of knowledge: The case of radical education discourse', *Qualitative Studies in Education*, **2**, pp. 131–44.

Grace, G. (1987), 'Teachers and the State in Britain: A changing relation', in Lawn, M. and Grace, G. (eds), *Teachers: The Culture and Politics of Work*, Sussex, Falmer Press.

Grant, G. (1988), 'Teacher Knowledge and Classroom Organization: Managing Critical Thinking Tasks', paper presented at the annual meeting of the American Educational Research Association, New Orleans.

Griggs, C. (1991), 'The National Union of Teachers in the Eastbourne area, 1874–1916: A tale of fact and pragmatism', *History of Education*, **20**, (4), pp. 325–40.

Hall, S. and Jaques, M. (1983), *The Politics of Thatcherism*, London, Lawrence & Wisehart.

Halmos, P. (1970), *The Personal Service Society*, London, Constable.

Hanson, E. Mark (1979), *Educational Administration and Organizational Behaviour*, Boston, Allyn & Bacon.

Hargreaves, A. and Dawe, R. (1990), 'Paths of professional development: Contrived collegiality, collaborative cultures and the case of peer coaching', *Teaching and Teacher Education*, **6**, (3), pp. 227–41.

Hargreaves, D. (1989), 'PGCE assessment fails the test', *Times Educational Supplement*, 6 October.

Hargreaves, D. (1992), 'The new professionalism', paper given to the

Fourth International Symposium: 'Teachers' Learning and School Development', University of New England, Northern Rivers, NSW, Australia, July 1992.

Hargreaves, D. and Hopkins, D. (1991), *The Empowered School*, London, Cassell.

Hartley, D. (1991), 'Democracy, capitalism and the reform of teacher education', *Journal of Education for Teaching*, **17**, (1), pp. 81–97.

Haug, M. (1973), 'Deprofessionalization: An alternative hypothesis for the future', in Halmos, P. (ed.), *Professionalization and Social Change* (Sociological Review Monograph 20), Keele, University of Keele.

Hillgate Group (1988), *Learning to Teach*, London, Claridge Press.

Hirst, P.H. (1984), 'Educational theory', in Hirst, P. (ed.), *Educational Theory and its Foundation Disciplines*, London, Routledge.

Hirst, P.H. (1990), 'The theory-practice relationship in teacher training', in Booth, M. *et al.* (eds), *Partnership in Initial Teacher Training*, London, Cassell.

Her Majesty's Inspectorate (HMI) (1980), *PGCE in the Public Sector*, London, HMSO.

HMI (1981), *Teacher Training in the Secondary School*, London, HMSO.

HMI (1982a), *Teacher Training and Preparation for Working Life*, London, HMSO.

HMI (1982b), *The New Teacher in School*, London, HMSO.

HMI (1983a), *Teaching Quality*, London, HMSO.

HMI (1983b), *Teaching in Schools: The Context of Initial Training*, London, HMSO.

HMI (1985), *Education Observed 3: Good Teachers*, London, HMSO.

HMI (1987), *Quality in Schools: The Initial Training of Teachers*, London, HMSO.

HMI (1988a), *Education Observed 7: Initial Teacher Training in the Universities*, London, HMSO.

HMI (1988b), *The New Teacher in School*, London, HMSO.

HMI (1990), *Perspectives on Teacher Education*, London, HMSO.

HMI (1991a), *The Professional Training of Primary School Teachers*, London, HMSO.

HMI (1991b), *School-Based Initial Training in England and Wales*, London, HMSO.

HMI (1991c), *Training Teachers for Inner City Schools*, London, HMSO.

Holmes Group (1986), *Tomorrow's Teachers: A Report of the Holmes Group*, East Lansing, Michigan, Holmes Group.

Hoyle, E. (1974), 'Professionality, professionalism and control in teaching', *London Educational Review*, **3**, (2).

Hoyle, E. (1980), 'Professionalization and deprofessionalization in education', in Hoyle, E. and Megarry, J. (eds), *The Professional Development* of Teachers: World Yearbook of Education, 1980, London, Kogan Page.

Hoyle, Eric (1986), The Politics of School Management, London, Hodder & Stoughton.

Hughes, E. (1958), Men and their Work, New York, Free Press.

Jackson, Philip W. (1968), Life in Classrooms, New York, Holt, Rinehart & Winston.

Jessop, B. et al. (1988), Thatcherism, Cambridge, Polity Press.

John, P.D. and Lucas, P. (eds) (1994), 'Progress and Partnership', University of Sheffield Division of Education Papers, 17, Sheffield, University of Sheffield Press.

Judge, H. (1980), 'Teaching professionalization: An essay in ambiguity', in Hoyle, E. and Megarry, J. (eds), World Yearbook of Education 1980: Professional Development of Teachers, London, Kogan Page.

Judge, H. (1989), 'The education of teachers in England and Wales', in Gumbert, E. (ed.), Fit to Teach: Teacher Education in International Perspective, Georgia, Georgia State University Press.

Kerchner, C.E. and Mitchell, D. (1988), The Changing Idea of a Teacher's Union, Sussex, Falmer Press.

Kerr, D. (1994), 'The Leicester Scheme', in John, P.D. and Lucas, P. (eds), Progress in Partnership, Sheffield, University of Sheffield Press.

Kyriacou, C. (1986), Effective Teaching in Schools, Oxford, Blackwell.

Lakoff, G. and Johnson, M. (1980), Metaphors We Live By, Chicago, University of Chicago Press.

Langford, Glenn (1985), Education, Persons and Society, London, Macmillan.

Larson, M.S. (1977), The Rise of Professionalism: A Sociological Analysis, Berkeley, University of California Press.

Lawlor, S. (1992), Teachers Mistaught, London, Centre for Policy Studies.

Lawn, M. (1987), Servants of the State: The Contested Control of Teaching, 1910–1930, Sussex, Falmer Press.

Lawn, M. and Ozga, J. (1986), 'Unequal partners: Teachers under indirect rule', British Journal of Sociology of Education, 7, (2).

Leinhardt, G. and Smith, D. (1985), 'Expertise in mathematics instruction: Subject matter knowledge', Journal of Educational Psychology, 77, pp. 247–71.

Lewin, K. (1946), 'Action research and minority problems', in Lewin, G.W. (ed.), Resolving Social Conflicts: Selected Papers on Group Dynamics, New York, Harper.

Lieberman, M. (1956), Education as a Profession, Englewood Cliffs, N.J., Prentice-Hall.

Lindley, R. (1986), Autonomy, London, Macmillan.

Liston, D.P. and Zeichner, K.M. (1988), Teacher Education and the

Social Conditions of Schooling, New York, Routledge.

Liston, D.P. and Zeichner, K.M. (1990), 'Reflective teaching and action research in pre-service teacher education', *Journal of Education for Teaching*, **16**, (3), pp. 235–54.

Little, J.W. (1990), 'The persistence of privacy: Autonomy and initiative in teachers' professional relations', *Teachers' College Record*, **91**, (4), pp. 509–36.

Lortie, D.C. (1964), 'The teacher and team teaching', in Shaplin, J.S. and Olds, H. (eds), *Team Teaching*, New York, Harper & Row.

Lortie, D. (1975), *Schoolteacher: A Sociological Study*, Chicago, University of Chicago Press.

Lowe, R. (1989), *Education in the Post-war Years: A Social History*, London, Routledge.

MacDonald, John (1970), *The Discernible Teacher*, Ottawa, The Canadian Teachers' Federation.

McIntyre, D. (1992), 'Theory, theorising and reflection in teacher education', in Calderhead, J. and Gates, P. (eds), *Conceptualising Reflection in Teacher Development*, Sussex, Falmer Press.

Maclure, S. (1978), 'Background to the accountability debate', in Becher, Tony and Maclure, Stuart (eds), *Accountability in Education*, Windsor, NFER Publishing Co.

McCutcheon, G. (1981), 'On the interpretation of classroom observation', *Education Researcher*, **10**, (5), pp. 5–10.

McNamara, D. (1990), 'The National Curriculum: An agenda for research', *British Educational Research Journal*, **16**, (30), pp. 225–35.

McNamara, D. (1992), 'The reform of teacher education in England and Wales: Teacher competence: panacea or rhetoric?', *Journal of Education for Teaching*, **18**, (3), pp. 273–87.

McNamara, D. and Desforges, C. (1978), 'The social sciences, teacher education and the objectification of craft knowledge', *British Journal of Teacher Education*, **4**, (1), pp. 17–36.

Manzer, R.A. (1970), *Teachers and Politics*, Manchester, Manchester University Press.

March, J.G. and Olsen, J.P. (eds) (1976), *Ambiguity and Choice in Organization*, New York, Free Press.

Millerson, G. (1964), *The Qualifying Associations*, London, Routledge.

Musgrave, P.W. (1970), 'A model for the analysis of the development of the English educational system from 1860', in Musgrave, P.W. (ed.), *Sociology, History and Education*, London, Methuen.

NCC (National Curriculum Council) (1991), *The National Curriculum and the Initial Training of Student, Articled and Licensed Teachers*, York, NCC.

Nias, J. (1989), *Primary Teachers Talking: A Study of Teaching as Work*, London, Routledge.

Nias, J. *et al.* (1989), *Staff Relationships in the Primary School*, London, Cassell.

Oakshott, M. (1962), *Rationales in Politics and Other Essays*, London, Methuen.

O'Connor, J. (1973), *The Fiscal Crisis of the State*, New York, St Martin's Press.

Office for Standards in Education (OFSTED) (1993), *The Articled Teacher Scheme*, London, HMSO.

(OFSTED) (1993), *The Licensed Teacher Scheme*, London, HMSO.

(OFSTED) (1993), *The New Teacher in School*, London, HMSO.

(OFSTED) (1993), *The Training of Primary School Teachers*, London, HMSO.

O'Hear, A. (1988), *Who Teaches the Teachers?*, London, Social Affairs Unit.

Ozga, J. (1988), 'Introduction: Teaching, professionalism and work', in Qzga, J. (ed.), *Schoolwork: Approaches to the Labour Process of Teaching*, Milton Keynes, Open University Press.

Ozga, J. (1992), 'An Education Profession for Tomorrow', paper presented at the Annual Conference of the Bristol Educational Management and Administration Society.

Ozga, J. and Lawn, M. (1981), *Teachers, Professionalism and Class*, Lewes, Falmer Press.

Parsons, Talcott (1954), *Essays in Sociological Theory* (Revised Edition), Glencoe, Free Press.

Pateman, Trevor (1978), 'Accountability, values and schooling', in Becher, T. and Maclure, S. (eds), *Accountability in Education*, Windsor, NFER Publishing Co.

Pearson, A.T. (1989), *The Teacher: Theory and Practice in Teacher Education*, New York, Routledge.

Pearson, L.C. and Hall, B.W. (1993), 'Initial construct validation of a teaching autonomy scale', *Journal of Educational Research*, **86**, (3), pp. 172–8.

Perkin, H. (1989), *The Rise of Professional Society*, London, Routledge.

Pinar, W. (1988), 'Autobiography and the architecture of the self', *Journal of Curriculum Theorizing*, **8**, (1), pp. 7–36.

Ranson, S. (1993), 'Markets or democracy for education?', *British Journal of Education Studies*, **41**, (4), pp. 333–53.

Reynolds, M.C. (ed.) (1989), *Knowledge Base for the Beginning Teacher*, New York, Pergamon.

Schon, Donald (1983), *The Reflective Practitioner*, New York, Basic Books.

Schon, Donald (1987), *Educating the Reflective Practitioner*, San Francisco, Jossey-Bass.

Short, E.C. (1985), 'The concept of competence: Its use and misuse in education', *Journal of Teacher Education*, (March), pp. 2–6.

Shulman, L.S. (1983), 'Autonomy and obligation', in Shulman, L.S. and Sykes, G. (eds), *Handbook of Teaching and Policy*, New York, Longman.

Shulman, L.S. (1987), 'Knowledge and teaching: Foundations of the New Reform', *Harvard Educational Review*, 57, pp. 1–22.

Smyth, John (1991), 'International perspectives on teacher collegiality: A labour process discussion based on the concept of teachers' work', *British Journal of Sociology of Education*, 12, (3).

Stenhouse, L. (1975), *An Introduction to Curriculum Research and Development*, London, Heinemann.

Swales, J.M. (1990), *Genre Analysis: English in Academic and Research Settings*, Cambridge, Cambridge University Press.

Taylor, W. (1984a), 'Metaphors of educational discourse', in Taylor, W. (ed.), *Metaphors of Education*, London, Heinemann.

Taylor, W. (1984b), 'The national context', in Alexander, R. *et al.* (eds), *Change in Teacher Education: Context and Provision Since Robbins*, London, Holt, Rinehart & Winston.

Thomas, W.I. and Znaniecki, F. (1939), *The Polish Peasant in Europe and America*, New York, Social Science Research Council.

Tom, A. (1992), 'Whither the Professional Curriculum for Teachers', *Review of Education*, 14, pp. 21–30.

Tropp, A. (1957), *The Schoolteachers*, London, Heinemann.

Tropp, A. (1970), 'The changing status of the teacher in England and Wales' in Musgrove, P.W. (ed.), *Sociology, History and Education*, London, Methuen.

Tyler, William (1988), *School Organization: A Sociological Perspective*, London, Croom Helm.

UCET (Universities Council for the Education of Teachers) (1979), *The PGCE Course and the Training of Specialist Teachers in Secondary Schools*, London, UCET.

Urban, W.J. (1990), 'Historical studies of teacher education', in Houston, R. (ed.), *Handbook of Research on Teacher Education*, New York, Macmillan.

Wardle, D. (1974), *The Rise of the Schooled Society*, London, Routledge.

Warnock, Mary (1977), in *Report of the Committee on the Future of Broadcasting* (Annan Report), HMSO, Cmnd. 6753, para. 4, 11.

Weick, K. (1976), 'Educational organizations as loosely-coupled systems', *Administrative Science Quarterly*, 21.

White, J. (1990), *Education and the Good Life*, London, Kogan Page.

Wilkin, M. (1990), 'The development of partnership in the United Kingdom', in Booth, M. *et al.* (eds), *Partnership in Initial Teacher Training*, London, Cassell.

Wilson, S. *et al.* (1987), '150 ways of knowing: Representations of knowledge in teaching', in Calderhead, J. (ed.), *Exploring Teachers' Thinking*, London, Cassell.

Woods, P. (1987), 'Life histories and teacher knowledge', in Smyth, J. (ed.), *Educating Teachers: Changing the Nature of Pedagogical Knowledge*, Sussex, Falmer Press.

Wragg, E.C. (1993), *Primary Teaching Skills*, London, Routledge.

Yinger, R. (1987), 'Learning the language of practice', *Curriculum Inquiry*, **17**, (3), pp. 293–317.

Index